PELÉ

MATT & TOM OLDFIELD

CLASSIC FOOTBALL HEROES

PELÉ

FROM THE PLAYGROUND
TO THE PITCH

DINO

First published by Dino Books in 2024,
an imprint of Bonnier Books UK,
4th Floor, Victoria House, Bloomsbury Square, London WC1B 4DA
Owned by Bonnier Books,
Sveavägen 56, Stockholm, Sweden

X @UFHbooks
X @footieheroesbks
www.heroesfootball.com
www.bonnierbooks.co.uk

Text © Studio Press 2024

Design by www.envydesign.co.uk

Paperback ISBN: 978 1 78946 756 7
E-book ISBN: 978 1 78946 768 0

British Library cataloguing-in-publication data:
A catalogue record for this book is available from the British Library.

Printed and bound in Great Britain by Clays Ltd, Elcograf S.p.A.

3 5 7 9 10 8 6 4 2

For Noah

*A big thank you for your help with research
and for being one of the first proofreaders.
We look forward to seeing more of your
Pelé magic on the pitch.*

Matt Oldfield is a children's author focusing on the wonderful world of football. His other books include *Unbelievable Football* (winner of the 2020 Children's Sports Book of the Year) and the *Johnny Ball: Football Genius* series. In association with his writing, Matt also delivers writing workshops in schools.

Cover illustration by Dan Leydon.
To learn more about Dan, visit danleydon.com
To purchase his artwork visit etsy.com/shop/footynews
Or just follow him on X @danleydon

TABLE OF CONTENTS

ACKNOWLEDGEMENTS

First of all I'd like to thank everyone at Bonnier Books
for supporting me and for running the ever-expanding
UFH ship so smoothly. Writing stories for the next
generation of football fans is both an honour and a
pleasure. Thanks also to my agent, Nick Walters, for
helping to keep my dream job going, year after year.

Next up, an extra big cheer for all the teachers,
booksellers and librarians who have championed these
books, and, of course, for the readers. The success of
this series is truly down to you.

Okay, onto friends and family. I wouldn't be writing
this series if it wasn't for my brother Tom. I owe him
so much and I'm very grateful for his belief in me
as an author. I'm also very grateful to the rest of my

family, especially Mel, Noah, Nico, and of course Mum and Dad. To my parents, I owe my biggest passions: football and books. They're a real inspiration for everything I do.

CHAPTER 1

THE RETURN OF THE KING

Estadio Azteca, Mexico City, 21 June 1970

Pelé had slept poorly the night before. There had been too many thoughts flying through his head.

It was the day of the 1970 World Cup Final – Brazil vs Italy – potentially the biggest day of his life. Fans across the globe would be watching and millions of Brazilians would be counting on him to deliver another trophy. Yes, that was the kind of pressure and excitement which had been keeping him awake.

From the very start, this tournament had been about two things for Pelé: putting smiles on the faces of everyone back home in Brazil and leaving his mark on his last World Cup. Now, he was just ninety minutes away from making both of those dreams a reality.

The last year had been a blur, starting from the moment that he agreed to return to the Brazil squad for the tournament, having already stepped away from international football following the 1966 World Cup. That tournament had ended in disappointing, bruising elimination for Brazil in the group stage – but now Pelé was back, in Mexico for one more chance at recapturing the Jules Rimet trophy.

Having finally drifted off to sleep, Pelé woke up in the morning with a burst of energy and determination flowing through his body. He took a deep breath and opened the curtains to let the morning sunshine in.

'It looks like the perfect day to win a World Cup,' he said to himself, smiling.

As he joined his teammates for breakfast, then later for the bus ride to the stadium, Pelé sensed the same mix of nervous energy and quiet confidence. But his swirling emotions were still there and his stomach was doing backflips.

Walking into the dressing room with what he hoped was a calming grin, he shook hands with Rivellino and Jairzinho, who had been alongside him through all the battles at this tournament.

'We're following your lead, King ,' Rivellino said, patting Pelé on the shoulder. 'Let's bring this trophy home.'

'Don't worry, we're going to make this the perfect ending,' Jairzinho added. 'That's what you deserve.'

'You guys are the best,' Pelé replied, his voice choking up with emotion.

The roar of the crowd gave Pelé goosebumps as the teams walked onto the pitch, and he was even more fired up when he stood next to his Brazil teammates for the national anthem.

'It's time for one more World Cup show!' Zagallo called out when Pelé jogged over to the touchline to get a ball.

Pelé winked. 'That's the plan!' he replied.

He knew that Italy would be using a few different tactics to slow him down and frustrate him. It was the obvious strategy. Sure enough, when he got his first touch, two or three Italian defenders swarmed around him before he could set off on a mazy run.

Then Brazil won a throw-in on the left wing, just in front of the corner flag. The throw-in dropped to Rivellino but an Italy defender rushed towards him. Rivellino just had time to loop a hopeful cross into the box, and Pelé instantly saw where it was going to land.

He took a few quick steps towards the back post and jumped as high as he could while keeping both eyes on the ball. He got up higher than his marker and thumped a powerful downward header past the Italy goalkeeper and into the bottom corner.

Gooooooooooooooooooooaaaaaaaaaaaaaaaaalllllllllllllll llllllllllll!!!!!!!!!!!!!!!!!!!!

Pelé was on the ground but he looked up to see the ball in the back of the net. He felt a sudden rush of joy and jumped up to celebrate. 'Let's go!!!!' he screamed.

Jairzinho rushed over to lift him into the air, and the rest of the team buried him in hugs.

'Unstoppable!' Rivellino shouted over the roar of the crowd. 'King Pelé does it again!'

Pelé felt like he was walking on air as he made his

way back to the halfway line. What a feeling! The fans were screaming, cheering and sharing in the joy of seeing another special Pelé moment. There was a buzz around the stadium every time he got the ball, and Italy were struggling to handle the speed and trickery of each Brazilian attack.

But a defensive mistake gifted Italy an equaliser and suddenly it was 1–1.

'It's okay!' Pelé called, clapping and encouraging his teammates after seeing a few nervous faces among the team's defenders. 'We'll get another goal.'

Brazil pushed forward again. Pelé went close with a chance at the back post, then Gérson thumped a shot into the net from the edge of the penalty area. 2–1.

Pelé leapt in the air. 'What a strike!' he screamed, feeling the relief of taking the lead again. They were back on track and hungry for more goals.

While Gérson prepared to take a free kick near the halfway line, Pelé started making a run and pointed to where he wanted the pass. When the referee blew the whistle, Gérson floated the ball over the Italian defence and Pelé was a step ahead.

It would have been reasonable to try to score another header or control the ball for a shot, but Pelé always had a clear picture of everything around him. Out of the corner of his eye, he saw Jairzinho sprinting into the box and he cushioned a header towards him. Jairzinho was almost running too fast and he scuffed his shot a little, but it was enough to wrong-foot the goalkeeper. The ball trickled into the net. 3–1.

Pelé could see some of the Italy players holding their heads or hunched over with their hands on their knees. It was a long way back for them now.

'Let's pass, move and keep the ball,' he said to Rivellino and Gérson back near the halfway line. 'We're so close now!'

He knew that they just had to let the minutes tick away. Brazil moved forward from the back again, passing down the left wing. Jairzinho collected a long pass, cut inside and laid the ball off to Pelé.

Again, Pelé knew exactly what he wanted to do before the ball even got to him. He could sense captain Carlos Alberto racing forward from right-back and he calmly rolled a pass to him. It was the perfect speed – not too fast, not too slow, and Carlos Alberto hit his shot first-time, arrowing it into the bottom corner. 4–1.

Now the party could really start! It was a beautiful goal to cap off a beautiful performance from a team that had played beautiful football throughout the tournament. At the final whistle, fans poured onto the pitch.

Before he even had a chance to raise his arms in celebration, Pelé was surrounded by fans, teammates and even a few of the Italy players. People congratulated him with hugs and handshakes, and some wanted his shirt, his shorts and his boots. His shirt was the first to go, and then his teammates lifted him onto their shoulders and carried him on a lap of the stadium. They all knew what it meant to him to be on top of the world again.

Confetti floated down from the roof of the stadium as Pelé followed Carlos Alberto up the steps to receive the trophy. There it was! The World Cup trophy, shining and golden, ready to be passed around the Brazil team.

At last, Pelé had the trophy in his hands. He just stared at it, with the biggest of smiles. He had allowed himself to picture this moment, reunited with the greatest prize of all for the third time, but none of that came close to the pride and happiness he felt now. The crowd was chanting his name again, with Brazil flags everywhere.

He hugged Zagallo as the team huddled together on the pitch. 'We did it!' Pelé said. 'Brazil are champions again!'

As the players boarded the plane home, they knew there were lots more celebrations ahead. For now, though, Pelé was happy enough to lean his head back in his seat, close his eyes and think about his remarkable football life.

CHAPTER 2

LITTLE EDSON'S BRIGHT FUTURE

Before those days when the nickname 'Pelé' followed him everywhere he went, he was simply Edson. Or Edson Arantes do Nascimento, to be precise.

He was born in October 1940 and his parents, Celeste and Dondinho, named him after Thomas Edison, the inventor of the lightbulb. They brought him home to their small house in Três Corações, a village north of Rio de Janeiro in Brazil, for the start of a whole new chapter.

Now they had a child to look after – and food and clothes to buy. But money was tight. Dondinho was playing in the local football league and earning just a small wage, though he was still dreaming of his big break with a top Brazilian club.

Celeste supported that dream too, but that didn't mean she was ready for Edson to follow the same path.

As tiny Edson lay on the bed and kicked his legs, Dondinho laughed.

'He's got the look of a footballer!' he announced proudly, turning to smile at Celeste, then stopping when he saw the frown on her face.

'Oh really?!' Celeste said, shaking her head while trying to hide a smile.

'Or, you know, something else where you need strong legs,' Dondinho added quickly, before changing the subject.

The family made the best out of everything, just eating the simplest of meals and making clothes last as long as possible. Of course, to little Edson, their home looked like so many others in Três Corações. That was the town he knew, and he had no idea that other parts of Brazil were richer, cleaner and safer.

One evening, Dondinho arrived home from his latest league game and sat down in a chair next to where his son was playing. Edson looked round as his dad picked up a little toy ball from the floor, threw it into the air and let it bounce off his head.

Edson giggled as he watched.

'Do you know how many headers I scored like that today, Edson?' Dondinho asked, repeating the trick.

Edson was too young to really understand what his father was asking him, so he just looked at him and grinned.

Dondinho took his son's hand and counted on his little fingers. 'One, two, three, four, five,' he said slowly. 'Five headers. Five goals. In one game.'

'Five,' Edson repeated, smiling and clapping.

'I jumped so high, higher than anyone else,' Dondinho added. 'It was like I was flying.'

Edson wobbled his way over to his dad for a hug.

'One day, maybe you're going to be a great goalscorer too,' Dondinho whispered, having learned his lesson about saying these things in front of his wife. 'You could play in the biggest stadiums against the best teams. You'll see, there's nothing better than scoring a goal, hearing the roar of the crowd and the fans singing your name.'

Soon the house got more crowded after Edson's little brother, Zoca, was born. Zoca was too little to join in with any ball games, but he liked to watch Edson dribbling the toy ball around the room or kicking it in the street with Dondinho and some of the neighbours.

Edson's parents always told him that anything was possible if he worked hard enough, but he would quickly learn that there were no guarantees, especially in football. Dondinho's career took a winding path with highs and lows and with various different clubs. Before long, the family was swapping Três Corações for São Lourenço. Then Dondinho changed teams again, so they packed up and moved to Lorena.

One sunny evening, Celeste brought Edson, Zoca and their new little sister Maria Lucia to watch their dad's game.

'We can only stay for the first half,' Celeste explained. 'Then it's bedtime. I don't want to hear any complaining when it's time to leave.'

Edson nodded. He had been looking forward to this

all day and he would do whatever he was told. He just wanted to see some of the game, and his eyes were instantly drawn to the freshly cut pitch and the crisp white lines. It seemed like paradise.

Then a long clearance bounced off the pitch and rolled towards Edson. He stopped it with his foot and kicked it towards the player who was jogging over to take the throw-in.

'Nice one!' the player called out, giving Edson a thumbs up as he picked up the ball.

Edson beamed and was soon telling the story to anyone who would listen.

Despite moving from town to town, Edson always seemed to have a smile on his face. He could deal with all of the change around him as long as he had his family and a ball to play with – and that made life easier, because they would all soon be on the move again.

CHAPTER 3

A NEW START IN BAURU

The train station was crowded and noisy. As Edson looked around, he saw people everywhere. It was a hot, dusty day and he could feel the sweat rolling down his back.

They were on their way to Bauru where Dondinho would be starting a new job. Well, two jobs really – playing football and working in an office.

His parents were standing next to the suitcases, with the train tickets in their hands. 'Two more minutes,' Celeste called, guessing that her son might have ideas about exploring. 'Stay close to us, Edson.'

Edson couldn't see much with the big crowd waiting on the platform, but he heard the train as it got nearer.

Standing on tiptoes, he saw the steam from the train floating up towards the sky, and then there was a big enough gap for him to see through. The train was huge! Once it had slowed to a stop, Edson climbed the small steps with his parents, Zoca and Maria Lucia.

'Ready for our big adventure?' Dondinho asked once they were all sitting down.

Edson grinned and nodded. He was already loving it and the train hadn't even left the station yet!

He watched the towns and villages as the train chugged slowly towards Bauru. Every few minutes, he had questions for his parents. 'What's that?' 'How does that work?' 'Where are we now?'

Celeste and Dondinho smiled as they watched their eldest son mesmerised by all the sights and sounds of the journey. This was going to be a big, scary change but the new job meant more money for food, clothes and a nice home. The opportunity was too good to turn down.

Edson had tried to picture what Bauru would be like, but it was impossible. He was only four years old and he had only ever seen the streets close to the family's homes in Três Corações, São Lourenço and Lorena.

When they finally arrived in Bauru, Edson's first thought was that it was a land for giants. There were so many tall buildings and he felt tiny looking up at them – and there were people everywhere. He almost got knocked off his feet twice, while just walking down the platform.

Trying to take in all the faces and places as they walked, Edson clung onto his mum's hand until they reached the nearby hotel where they would be staying until they decided on a more permanent home. It had been a long day and they were all looking forward to a good night's sleep.

The first few months in Bauru brought a mix of good news and bad news. While the office job fell through, things went much more smoothly on the football pitch.

'Can I come with you?' Edson asked excitedly one morning as Dondinho carried his plate to the sink. Whenever he was allowed, Edson loved to tag along for his dad's games or training sessions.

Dondinho was playing for Bauru Athletic Club, or BAC, and he had made a good start as the team's new striker. It wasn't the top tier of Brazilian football but it was a good standard, with nice stadiums and pitches that were carefully looked after.

No one cheered louder than Edson as he watched every pass, tackle and shot from the stands. Being a footballer seemed like the best job in the world. He seemed to be a lucky charm too. Bauru kept winning, Dondinho kept scoring and BAC were soon local cup champions.

Edson wasn't the only Dondinho fan either. More and more often, BAC supporters would recognise Dondinho in the street and rush over to shake his hand, while Edson and Zoca giggled.

'Great goal on Saturday!'

'Good luck at the weekend!'

Edson quickly became a regular in the BAC dressing room. At first, he was shy and didn't know what to say, but once he had spoken to his dad's teammates a few times, he felt like part of the team. He soaked it all in – the football talk, the smells, the laughter, the energy. He saw how happy the players were after a win, and how disappointed everyone looked after a loss.

Edson didn't even mind that no one could remember his name. Instead, the players just called him 'Dondinho's son', high-fiving him and patting his head as he skipped and weaved around the dressing room.

'Your son's got some moves, Dondinho!' one of the players shouted as Edson tried a few keepy-ups in the corner.

'He'll be taking your place up front soon!' added another.

Edson learned a lot from watching those BAC games. He immediately noticed how quickly the players moved the ball up and down the pitch, and the different techniques they used to control passes.

But he saw much more than that too. He could see who was in space and who was making a run. His brain took all that information and picked out the next move, and the one after that. He didn't realise it at the time, but it was one of the first signs that he had a special gift as a footballer.

'Did you enjoy the game today?' Dondinho asked one night after he and Celeste had told a story to their three children.

Edson nodded with a big smile. 'Watching your games is always really fun,' he said. 'When I'm older, I want to be just like you!'

CHAPTER 4

CALL HIM "PELÉ"

His days of being Edson didn't last much longer.
Brazilians love their nicknames and his family were
soon calling him 'Dico', a name that Uncle Jorge, a
regular guest at their house, had given him.

But he was about to get another nickname that
would later become known all around the world.

The school playground in Bauru had goalposts
painted onto the wall, and Edson made the most
of every minute to play football – before school,
at lunchtime and after school. His teachers always
knew where to find him if he was late getting to
his classroom.

One afternoon, after the school day was over, Edson

borrowed one of the school's old balls and dribbled into the playground to squeeze in some more shooting practice with his friends, Ze Roberto and Vadinho.

When he was tired of firing shots at the goal, Edson took over as the goalkeeper and let Ze Roberto and Vadinho have a turn. He always quite liked the pressure of being the keeper.

The first few shots flew wide, then the third one curled towards him. Edson dived and pushed the ball away.

'What a save from Bilé!' Edson shouted, remembering the keeper who he had played with Dondinho earlier in his career and had become a personal favourite.

Ze Roberto laughed. 'Who? Pelé?' he asked.

'No, it's Bilé,' Edson said again. He had settled well in Bauru but still had a slightly different accent. 'He's one of the best goalkeepers I've ever seen. He used to play for my dad's team and he always made amazing saves.'

A few other boys had joined in now, passing the ball back and forth before taking a shot.

'Okay, well if he's Bilé, you can be Pelé,' Ze Roberto replied. 'That's what it sounded like anyway.'

'What does Pelé mean?' asked Vadinho, looking confused.

'I was just going to ask the same thing,' added Ari, another friend from his class.

Ze Roberto shrugged and they all started laughing.

As Edson walked home that night, he was sure that the nickname would be forgotten by the time he got to school the next day. It wasn't as if the name had any real connection to him.

But he was wrong. Word had spread, and several voices called out 'Pelé!' as they ran over to see him in the playground the next morning. 'Oh, great,' he said to himself, rolling his eyes.

That evening, Celeste laid out plates on the table ready for dinner, and then picked up five forks. 'Dico, come and put these on the table,' she called. Her son appeared in the kitchen.

'Oh, I forgot to tell you, I've got a new name,' he explained, picking up the plates carefully. 'I'm Dico at home, but apparently I'm now Pelé at school!'

'Oh, right,' Celeste said, laughing.

'What's a "Pelé"?' Zoca asked, turning around in his chair and looking at Celeste for the answer.

'No idea!' Celeste said. 'It's the first time I've ever heard it.'

Like so many nicknames, it was annoying at first. Of course, as soon as the other boys saw that the name got a reaction from Edson, they used it even more! Eventually, though, he started to like it. He was scoring more goals than ever at the moment, so maybe 'Pelé' was actually good luck.

Later that week, the group of friends were sorting out teams for a quick game with some neighbours from a few streets away. One boy arrived a few minutes late and asked to join in.

'Sure, you can join Dico's team,' Zoca said, using his usual nickname for his brother.

'Who?' the little boy asked, looking confused.

'Dico,' Zoca repeated, pointing. 'He's the skinny one over there.'

'Just call him Pelé!' shouted Ze Roberto, and Vadinho and Ari laughed. 'That's his new name!'

As the game began, the ball bounced loose – and Vadinho started commentating loudly from further up the pitch.

'Pelé gets the ball,' he called out. 'He dribbles past one defender and plays the one-two with Ze Roberto. What a move! Pelé flicks the ball up and… wow, what a shot! Goal for Pelé!'

It was the first time that a 'commentator' had described a Pelé goal – and it certainly wouldn't be the last.

CHAPTER 5

THE PERFECT SHINE

With family and friends around them, Bauru was
starting to feel like home for Celeste and Dondinho,
and they had adjusted to how much bigger it was than
Três Corações or the other towns where they had lived.
Pelé (he was really liking the name now) had settled
into life at Ernesto Monte primary school, though his
teachers were desperate for him to work harder.

But then disaster struck, shaking them all out of that
peacefulness. In BAC's next game, Dondinho twisted
awkwardly as he reached for a pass and he fell to the
ground holding his knee. He had to be helped off the
pitch by his teammates and a doctor was called to do a
closer examination.

It was bad news – a serious knee injury that required rest and a lengthy recovery. The message was clear: Dondinho had to rest at home and let the injury heal if he wanted to get back on the pitch any time soon.

Pelé didn't know what to say. He could see the pain and frustration on his dad's face as he sat in his favourite chair, propping up his leg on a box. Pelé brought him ice and wished there was more that he could do to help.

Worse of all, without the football wages, the money worries returned for Celeste and Dondinho – and this time, Pelé was old enough to understand the situation they were in. Scary questions floated through his head. Would they have to move again? Would there be enough food to eat?

A few weeks after Dondinho's injury, Pelé had an idea that he hoped might take away a little of their worry. Now he just needed to convince his parents.

After dinner, he hurried out of the room and came back with an old brush and a couple of torn rags. 'I'm going to earn some money shining shoes,' he announced.

His parents looked at each other. This was quite a surprise. But then Celeste shook her head.

'We love that you want to help,' she said, gently. 'But you're only seven and it's not fair to ask you to do that. We're going to find another way.'

'But I *want* to do it and I'll be careful,' Pelé said, pleading with his most angelic face. 'Please, let me give it a try.'

'Celeste, you know how determined he is when he gets an idea like this,' Dondinho said quietly, with a half-smile. 'Maybe we can find a compromise so that he's nearby and safe.'

Eventually, they agreed that Pelé could set up his shoe-shining business in the streets close to their home, but he had to promise not to walk off into any other neighbourhoods.

Early the next morning, he bounced out of bed and got everything ready. He carried the supplies outside and waited patiently.

'Hello, sir!' he called out, waving one of the rags as a man in a suit walked towards him. 'Let's make those shoes a bit shinier!'

The man paused and smiled. 'Actually, that would be great for my meetings today, but I only have a few minutes.'

'That's all I need,' Pelé replied, grinning. He positioned his little wooden box for the man, who lifted his right foot onto the box. Pelé put a little polish on his rag and began shining the man's shoe.

Within minutes, the black shoes were sparkling. Pelé stood up and admired his work. His customer did the same.

'Great job!' the man said, picking up his briefcase and reaching into his pocket. He gave Pelé a handful of coins and hurried off down the street.

Jingling the coins in his hand, Pelé couldn't stop smiling. But his work wasn't done. He put the money away and looked out for more customers.

At the end of the day, he rushed home, getting back to the house in record time. He couldn't wait to tell everyone about his success.

'Mum, Dad, are you home?' he called out as soon as he had opened the door.

'What's wrong?' Celeste asked, running through

from the next room and fearing that her son had run into some trouble. 'Did something happen?'

'Well, yes, but only good things!' Pelé said, grinning. He opened his shoe-shining box and collected his pile of coins. He put them on the table, turning around just in time to see the shock on his parents' faces.

'Wow, son, that's amazing!' they both said, wrapping him in a hug.

Pelé picked a few more places where he thought business would be good, with lots of people walking past. It would still be a small price for each customer, but it could add up to a lot in the end. He even joined Dondinho, in continued injury recovery, in training sessions and found good business there.

When Dondinho finally put his football boots away for good, he found an office job instead. It was a steady position and meant that money – and food and clothes – wasn't such a scary topic anymore.

Pelé was relieved. Shining shoes was really hard work, but he was proud to have stepped up when his family needed him.

CHAPTER 6

SOCKS AND STRING

Even when he was taking on his shoe-shining
responsibilities, Pelé never missed a chance to join in
the street football games in their local neighbourhood.
As long as there was even a sliver of daylight, the
sounds of bouncing balls and running feet could be
heard around Rubens Arruda Street.

But it wasn't just the games themselves that were
competitive. There was even competition to have a
chance to play. At first, that meant asking the older
boys again and again if he could join the game.

It often didn't work in his favour, though. When
the older, bigger kids looked at Pelé, they saw a small,
skinny boy with no shoes. Surely he couldn't be good

at football, they thought. They sometimes said those things directly to his face, but that didn't shake Pelé's confidence at all. He knew he could match the older boys if he got the opportunity to prove it.

When he was finally allowed to play, Pelé tried to copy all the things he had learned from watching his dad in action. He took quick touches, keeping the ball close to his feet as he dodged in and out of clothes on washing lines, market stands and people walking in the street – and he tried to set up his teammates so that no one could accuse him of being selfish.

Ze Roberto, Vadinho and Ari joined him too whenever they were allowed. Zoca tagged along as well and was sometimes added to whichever team Pelé was on.

But soon Pelé and his friends decided it was time for them to have their own games – and have full control over whether they could play! There was one problem, though. They needed a ball.

There was no chance of collecting enough money to buy a ball – so they got creative, using an idea they had heard about from other boys in their neighbourhood. First, Pelé and Zoca brought any old paper or newspaper they could find and screwed it up into a big ball. Then Ze Roberto and Vadinho found some old socks. They filled one of the socks with paper and rolled up the other socks inside too.

Ari brought two long pieces of string and together they bundled the bulging sock into a round shape and tied it as tightly as they could. Pelé put it down on a table and they all crowded round to take a closer look. None of them knew whether this new 'ball' would be sturdy enough to survive a game in the street, but they were about to find out.

'Let's take it for a spin,' Vadinho said, tucking it under his arm and heading outside.

For a few minutes, they stood in a circle and kicked their new ball around. Most of the boys were playing without shoes, so they were all happy enough to use this softer ball. It got dirty within seconds, but the string didn't budge.

'Okay, who are you playing as?' Ze Roberto asked. 'My dad always says Ademir is his favourite Brazil player, so I'm going to be him.'

'I'm Zizinho,' Ari and Vadinho both said at the same time.

'Well, that's an easy one for me!' Pelé said, when everyone looked in his direction. 'I'm Dondinho!'

They found a few other boys from their school who lived in the same neighbourhood and soon a regular 5-on-5 game began in the evenings and at weekends.

It didn't take long for Pelé to stand out as the best player. He was just quicker than everyone else – and that wasn't only because he was the fastest runner. Every touch, every turn and every run happened at lightning speed. He could take a pass, lay it off, spring open again in space to get the ball back and spin away to set up another teammate.

Pelé loved to picture that he was playing on perfect green grass rather than a bumpy street. After he skipped past two tackles and scored with a quick shot, he put his hands in the air.

'Dondinho does it again!' he shouted, jumping up to high-five Zoca and Ze Roberto.

'Give us a chance!' Ari called out, laughing while trying to catch his breath.

With a few running repairs, and a few more rags and socks to make it a bit bigger, the ball remarkably survived weeks and weeks of intense games. It was hardly the special professional ball that Pelé and his friends had seen on posters, but it rolled just fine and it gave them the freedom to have their own matches. To them, that was all that mattered.

CHAPTER 7

SETE DE SETEMBRO

The more that Pelé played in the street games, the deeper his love of football became. It wasn't just the tricks and flicks that he liked practising, it was the fierce battle of each game. All the boys took it very seriously and hated to lose. Plenty of times, Pelé arrived home covered in mud and had to pour water on his knees and elbows to get them clean again. Still, it was always worth it.

'We're so much better than we used to be,' Vadinho said during their walk home from their latest tiring game.

'But how can we become a proper team?' Ze Roberto asked, running to catch up after collecting the old shoes they were using as goalposts.

'A real team costs money for kits and boots,' Ari replied. 'We have the skills and teamwork, but we don't have money.'

'Well, we'll have to work on that part,' Pelé admitted. 'But being a team is about more than just what we wear. While we're trying to raise some money, let's ask some of the other boys at school if they have teams or know other kids who play football. It wouldn't be a real team in a real league yet, but it could be fun.'

They all liked the sound of that, and soon all kinds of plans were in motion.

'So, what are we going to call our new team?' Vadinho asked at the end of one of their planning conversations at Pelé's house.

'What about Sete de Setembro?' Pelé replied. 'That's one of the streets where we started playing together.'

They all agreed that the name probably needed more work, but it was good enough for now.

Later that week, Pelé and Zoca were in the middle of their latest button football battle, a game where each player has eleven buttons and uses them to flick the ball towards the goal. Then Pelé stopped and moved a few of the extra buttons over to the far side of the table.

'What are you doing?' Zoca asked.

'After this game, let's use the buttons to see how we're going to play,' he said, grinning. 'Like, how many defenders? Three or four? What about in midfield?'

Zoca laughed but he couldn't resist getting involved. Dondinho heard the conversation and hurried over to give his ideas too.

'What about three midfielders here?' Pelé suggested, pointing and moving the buttons. 'Then a more attacking midfielder just behind me up front.'

'Maybe this is how all the great managers should plan their tactics,' Dondinho joked. 'Button football never gets it wrong!'

Soon, they were playing proper games every week. The Sete de Setembro boys weren't going to win any prizes for the kit they showed up wearing – usually barefoot with whichever old T-shirt and shorts they could find – but they rang rings around their opponents.

Even though a lot of the boys had played together in the street games, it took a little time to get used to each other's runs and playing proper positions. But that didn't slow them down for long, and they were just more talented than the rest of the local teams.

Their run of victories went on and on: 5–1, 6–2, 7–3, 8–0. No one could get near them, and Pelé was getting used to scoring a hat-trick in every game. From the very start, he was picked to be the team's main striker and, even without shoes, his shots were often unstoppable.

There was another reason for the boys' smiling faces too. By selling peanuts, they got enough money to buy matching shirts. Now they would look more like a real team – and somehow the new shirt seemed to make Pelé play even better.

'Get it to Pelé!' Ari shouted in the final minutes of a rare close game.

Vadinho quickly chipped the ball forward into space, and Pelé was onto it in a flash. He dribbled inside and saw a big defender hesitate after being left in the dust by Pelé twice already. He faked to go one direction, then poked the ball through the defender's legs and raced away.

Now it was Pelé in a one-on-one against the keeper. There was only going to be one winner. He raced on, waited patiently for the keeper to come rushing out, then flicked the ball round him and rolled it into the goal.

Goooooooooooooooooooaaaaaaaaaaaaaaaalllllllllllll llllllllllll!!!!!!!!!!!!!!!!!!!

Sete de Setembro quickly gained a reputation as one of the most skilful, talented local teams, and they were still training every week to stay sharp.

The next week, Pelé arrived at school just in time to see Ze Roberto weaving through a crowd of kids and racing towards him.

'A tournament!' Ze Roberto shouted, waving a sheet of paper that was getting really crumpled in his hand.

'Slow down!' Pelé said, laughing. 'What tournament?'

Ze Roberto panted and tried to catch his breath.

'The mayor is setting up a youth football tournament,' he finally managed to reply. 'It'll be here in Bauru and any local team can enter.'

Pelé's eyes lit up. A big tournament was just what they had been waiting for. They ran over to share the good news with Vadinho and Ari.

There was a lot of excitement in the air at the next Sete de Setembro training session. All the players had heard about the tournament and were counting the days until they would get to show what they could do in a real competition.

Pelé was always confident when it came to winning football games, but he especially liked Sete de Setembro's chances. They had beaten most of the other teams and he had even scored five goals against some of them.

For a while, it looked like the team would need to win the tournament with the same barefoot style – and they weren't even sure if that would be allowed. But then a local businessman came to the rescue, sponsoring the team so that, at last, all the players would have boots.

As the tournament kicked off, Dondinho took a ball into the street whenever he could and helped his son work on his control and his heading. Pelé could also feel he was getting stronger on his left foot, even though he could still kick it much harder and more accurately with his right foot.

'You need to use both feet,' Dondinho would remind him. 'That way, you're really unpredictable for defenders. They'll be terrified trying to guess where you're going to dribble.'

Sete de Setembro breezed through the first three rounds, with Pelé scoring two hat-tricks. Ze Roberto's tap-in was the winning goal in the quarter-finals and Pelé hit two screamers on the way to a 4–2 win in the semi-finals.

Now they had a nervous wait for the final. To make it a more special occasion, the game would be played at the main BAC stadium – and Pelé soon heard that tickets were selling fast.

'Well I guess I was right,' Dondinho said, smiling.

'About what?' Pelé asked.

'I always had a feeling that you would play at this

stadium, just like I used to,' Dondinho replied.

Pelé would never forget the feeling of walking onto the BAC pitch as a player. It was an unfamiliar feeling but a stadium he knew very well. The start of the game was a blur, with lots of nerves and everyone swept up in the excitement, but soon Sete de Setembro took control.

Defenders crowded around Pelé but he found ways to escape and set up his teammates. Ari and Vadinho scored goals from Pelé's passes, and Sete de Setembro hung on despite a nervy second half.

'Champions! Champions! Champions!' they all cheered as their friends and family joined them to celebrate. In that moment, they all felt like professional footballers. Soon another chant was floating around the stadium too. It started quietly, then got louder and louder.

'Pelé! Pelé! Pelé!'

As he looked round towards the main stand, Pelé couldn't believe what he was hearing.

'You're famous now, bro!' Zoca shouted, jumping on his brother's back as they waved to the crowd.

CHAPTER 8

THE PROMISE

The radio was turned up as loud as it would go, and Dondinho stretched nervously in his chair. The whole family had been waiting for this day – the 1950 World Cup Final, being played at the famous Maracanã Stadium in Brazil. Flags were flying, horns were blaring and everyone in the neighbourhood was getting ready for a big party.

Pelé sat on the floor, trying not to make any noise in case he distracted the grown-ups or made them miss an important moment. He was just happy to be part of it all.

Brazil and Uruguay were the last two teams standing, and most people were saying that Brazil would win. But that didn't seem to be helping anyone in the room feel more relaxed. Losing would be bad enough, but losing to another South American team would add an extra layer of pain.

Pelé could feel the tension around him and knew enough about football and the World Cup to understand what this game meant for the whole country. If they were all this nervous just listening to the game, Pelé wondered what it must be like for the players.

'There are going to be 170,000 people at the Maracanã today,' Dondinho said. 'It'll either be a massive party or a terrible nightmare.'

With a crackle, the radio commentator announced that the players were walking onto the pitch, and they could clearly hear the roar of the crowd.

Dondinho stood up and went to shake hands with each person for good luck. When he got to Pelé, he grinned and hugged him. 'Here we go!' he said.

Then the room went silent except for the radio. It was as if everyone was collectively holding their breath and waiting to see what would happen next.

When Brazil scored just after half-time, everyone screamed and jumped up, scaring Pelé for a second. He rushed to join in and heard fireworks fizzing in the sky around the neighbourhood.

'1–0 to Brazil!' Pelé shouted to the boys playing outside.

'We're playing well,' Dondinho said, tapping his hands on the side of his chair. 'But it's not over yet.'

'We need another goal before we can relax,' one of his friends agreed.

Pelé could tell that Brazil were having most of the chances. He kept hearing names he recognised from conversations with his dad or his friends: Ademir, Chico, Zizinho – and Friaça, who had scored the Brazil goal.

But the room fell silent again when Uruguay scored to make it 1–1. Brazil's advantage was gone. 'Come on boys!' Uncle Jorge shouted. 'Wake up!'

Then there was another groan – 2–1 to Uruguay. His dad and his uncles all had their own ideas about what was going wrong and how to fix it.

'We're giving this away!' they all said.

The minutes ticked by, and then the sound of the final whistle came through loud and clear on the radio. Uruguay had won.

'I can't believe it!' one of Dondinho's friends said, putting his head in his hands.

Pelé heard the commentators in shock, describing the emotions of the players and the mood in the stadium, which was now almost empty. There was sadness in their voices as they talked about this 'national tragedy'.

As Pelé got up to go back outside to see his friends, he suddenly noticed that his dad was crying.

'It's okay, Dad,' he said, putting his hand on Dondinho's shoulder. 'Brazil will have another chance at the next World Cup.'

Dondinho did his best to smile. 'You're right, son, but this should have been our tournament,' he said sadly. 'We let it slip away and that's what really hurts.'

'Don't worry,' Pelé replied. 'When I'm older, I promise I'll win a World Cup for you.'

That was enough to put a real smile on his dad's face – and for a second, Dondinho seemed to be picturing his son in the famous yellow Brazil shirt.

Pelé felt a little better as he left the room. He hadn't really thought much about playing for Brazil – it had just seemed like a nice thing to say to cheer up his dad. But now that he had said the words out loud, Pelé liked the sound of it.

CHAPTER 9

BAQUINHO BALLER

Although Dondinho's playing days were over now, he was still in touch with some of his old friends from his Bauro Athletic Club days. That meant it didn't take long for him to find out about some exciting new developments.

'I heard today that Bauro Athletic Club is starting a youth program,' Dondinho explained excitedly as the family sat down for supper one evening. 'That's going to be a game-changer for all the talented local players.'

That got Pelé's attention.

'This could be perfect for you,' Dondinho added, looking at his two sons. 'There will be lots of other kids there who love football, and the team will be playing on proper pitches so you'll get fewer cuts and bruises.'

Pelé still lived for the Sete de Setembro games and wanted to keep that going, but he was also ready to test himself in a real league.

'So, what happens next?' Celeste asked, trying to make sense of it all. 'I think we need more information before we can decide if it's a good idea.'

Pelé stayed silent. He already thought it was a good idea, but he knew it wasn't up to him to decide.

Dondinho came back with more details later that week. The team was called Baquinho and they would be holding a few trials to select the best players for the squad. Pelé was already counting down the days – and he was relieved that he could still fit into all of his Sete de Setembro kit, including his boots.

He arrived at the trial just in time to look around the group of boys. He spotted many that he knew from their street football battles. Then the Baquinho coaches took the boys through a quick warm-up and divided them into teams. There were two pitches marked out with cones and a couple of the coaches would be refereeing while the others took notes.

Pelé had been a bit scared about the idea of a trial, but he forgot all about that once he started playing. His first three touches were probably enough to get his name in the Baquinho team. He controlled a high pass effortlessly on his chest, let it drop to the ground at his right foot and flicked a pass to a teammate.

Then he ran forward to get into space again. A long pass came in his direction, along the floor this time. Pelé sensed a defender closing in behind him, so instead of controlling the ball and risking a strong tackle, he chose to dummy it. He let the pass go between his legs, then spun to chase after it.

That completely confused the defender and there was no way he was catching up. Pelé reached the ball in a flash and instantly thumped a shot past the keeper.

Goooooooooooooooooooooaaaaaaaaaaaaaaaaalllllllllllllll llllllllllll!!!!!!!!!!!!!!!!!!!!!!

Three touches, but one piece of magic after another.

That move was the highlight of the day, but Pelé went on to score more goals and set up a few for his teammates. He was exhausted as the coaches finally whistled for the end of the session. There would be a couple more trial sessions, the coaches explained, but some boys might be offered a contract sooner. Pelé was one of them.

After signing the Baquinho forms, which included a small wage, Pelé found out that his new head coach would be Waldemar de Brito, a former professional with several teams around the country, and who had also played eighteen games for Brazil.

Pelé thought he had heard that name before – and he was right. Dondinho knew all about Waldemar from his own playing days and had told him a few stories over the years.

'Waldemar is brilliant,' Dondinho explained as they arrived at the first proper training session. 'It's amazing for Baquinho to have him onboard with all his knowledge. You'll really like him.'

'There's great potential in this group,' Waldemar said, his loud voice echoing around the room. 'And we're going to work you all hard to help you reach that potential.'

All of the players sat completely still. None of them wanted to look like they weren't listening.

'I'm really excited to be here,' Waldemar continued, pacing over to the window and then back again. 'Even though we're a new team, I believe we can win against anyone. Who's ready to shake up the league?'

The boys all cheered.

Waldemar soon had the players working up a sweat, and every session was interesting and creative. Pelé could immediately see that everything at Baquinho would be run almost like a professional team.

Pelé worked on his finishing, especially with his left foot, and spent hours improving his heading. In all the mini games, he was a few steps ahead with his movement and his technique. He loved feeling part of the team and he took great pride in looking after the kit provided by the club.

Waldemar taught Pelé some important lessons, like his body position when receiving a pass, how to have the vision of what was around him and when to shoot and when to pass. Best of all, Pelé could really feel the improvements month after month.

He enjoyed working with his teammates and all the coaches in training, but he really came alive on gamedays. He was pumped up from the second he put on the Baquinho shirt, and defences rarely stood a chance.

Some players would have been thrilled to score one or two goals in a game, but that was never enough for Pelé. That season, he scored every type of goal imaginable – 148 goals in thirty-three games to be exact. There were headers and volleys, free kicks and penalties, back-heels and bicycle kicks as Baquinho powered past every opponent on the way to winning the 1954 Youth Championship.

The rest of Brazil was starting to take notice and there were soon whispers of scouts showing up to some of the BAC games. Before Pelé could even think about what that might mean for his career, Waldemar had a suggestion of his own. He and the other coaches knew that a few professional clubs were interested in Pelé, but he wanted to bring him for a trial at Santos first.

'He's got something special,' Waldemar had

explained to his contacts at Santos. 'Trust me, I don't say this often, but Pelé could go on to be the best player in the world.'

That was enough to get Santos interested and a trial was quickly arranged. Pelé would soon be travelling there for whatever adventures lay ahead. Life was moving so fast for him, but he liked where he was going.

CHAPTER 10

THE SANTOS DREAM

'Please stand still!' Celeste pleaded. She was trying to get the measurements right for her son's new trousers.

'Sorry,' Pelé said, quickly doing his best statue impression. 'I just keep thinking about things I need to do before the trip to Santos.'

Celeste's face changed from frustration to sadness. She looked at the floor. The idea of her son being far away was a scary thought, and she knew there were going to be a lot of tears when they took him to the train station later that week.

Pelé had his own concerns and doubts about the journey and the trial, but equally he knew it was too good an opportunity to turn down.

'You've always got to chase your dreams,' Uncle Jorge told him when they all gathered for one last meal before the trip. 'It won't always be easy, but never give up!'

Thankfully, Pelé wouldn't be going to Santos on his own. Dondinho was joining him, and then they would be meeting Waldemar on the way.

Finally, the day arrived and Pelé put the last few things in his suitcase. Sure enough, everyone was crying when he waved goodbye to Celeste, Zoca and Maria Lucia. But Pelé reminded himself that this was about his future – and his family's future. He would see them again soon.

Pelé and Dondinho met up with Waldemar for the second part of the journey to Santos. Pelé had been lucky enough to have lots of conversations with Waldemar at Baquinho, but this was an extra chance. They had hours to talk about football, and he wanted all the advice he could get before they arrived.

'If there's one thing I want you to remember, it's to be yourself,' Waldemar told him. 'Pretend you're playing with your friends in a street game or in one of our Baquinho matches rather than training with Santos. Don't let the pressure of a trial change the way you play, because you're at your best when you're having fun.'

Pelé had pictured that he would be unpacking and taking it easy for a couple of days until the trial started, but Waldemar had a surprise for them. He had three tickets for the Santos home game that weekend and then he brought Pelé to the dressing room to meet the players as well as the first team coach, Lula.

Now Pelé was really star-struck! He shook hands, said a few words and tried not to seem too shy. It helped that Santos had won that afternoon's game so everyone was in a good mood.

With so many football-obsessed youngsters in Brazil, it wasn't unusual for good players to come to Santos, but the club was on the lookout for *great* players. And the coaches saw that greatness in Pelé from the first few minutes of the first trial session.

The coaches exchanged grins and nods while they watched Pelé weave through tackles and fire unstoppable shots past whichever unlucky keeper was standing in the goal. Then there was some 'oohs' and 'aahs'. As the excitement grew on the touchline, Lula soon wandered over to see for himself.

Pelé left a defender on the floor, nutmegged another and calmly chipped the ball into the top corner.

Goooooooooooooooooooooaaaaaaaaaaaaaaaaalllllllllllllll llllllllllll!!!!!!!!!!!!!!!!!!!!!

There was no big celebration – he just jogged back and got ready to keep playing.

'We can't let him leave without signing for Santos,' Lula said, breaking the stunned silence and saying what they were all thinking.

'This kid could be in the first team in no time,' one of the coaches added. 'It doesn't matter if he's only fifteen. He's got a gift. You can see it with every touch.'

'Luckily, he's here with us for a few weeks,' another coach said. 'But we'll make sure this is a top priority.'

'Good, well let's get him training with the first team,' Lula said, catching the other coaches by surprise. 'I know we wouldn't normally do that for young players on trial, but I think we can make an exception here.'

Before long, and still just fifteen years old, Pelé was officially a Santos player and he had a paper contract in his hands to prove it. He knew from talking to Waldemar and a few of his new coaches that Santos had been through some tough years, with other bigger clubs in Brazil getting all the attention, like Corinthians, Palmeiras, Vasco da Gama and Flamengo.

That was the challenge that lay in front of him – putting Santos back on the map. From the minute he put on the white shirt and skipped up the steps to the training pitch, Pelé knew that he had made the right decision.

But he had to set reasonable expectations for himself. Obviously, he would love to play a big role, but he was still so young and it would take time to convince the coaches that he was ready for the physicality and pressure of first team football.

On top of all that, it had been really hard for Pelé to leave home and move away from his family. Santos wasn't too far from Bauru and he would be able to visit sometimes, but the distance still felt enormous for him. Still, having the ball at his feet was always a good distraction and the loneliness just made him work even harder.

Training with the first team was like a dream, as he shared the pitch with great Brazilian players like Jair, Formiga and Pepe. But Coach Lula was cautious about throwing his teenage star into games too often. Instead, Pelé played for the Under 18s and Under 20s at first, getting more experience, developing his skills, and growing a little taller. He helped the Under 20s team win the league championship and piled up goal after goal.

Lula made sure that Pelé still felt close to the first team, though, giving him some minutes in friendlies. He even got his first goal for Santos, firing in a rebound after Pepe's shot was saved.

Pelé had seen from training against grown men that he needed more muscle. He didn't like being knocked off the ball and he promised himself that he would get stronger. There was usually lots of food available at Santos and he made the most of every meal.

'Someone's been in the gym!' Pepe shouted, as Pelé

held off Formiga later in the year and scored in a one-on-one drill.

Pelé had done everything that the coaches had asked, and he could feel the big rewards were just around the corner.

CHAPTER 11

A WHOLE NEW LEVEL

Ahead of the 1957 season, summer training sessions were going well and the quality of their mini games was incredible. When Pelé got the tap on the shoulder from Coach Lula at the end of one particularly tiring session, he could feel his heart beating faster. Was this going to be good news or bad news? Lula's face gave nothing away.

'This is going to be a really important season for us,' Lula began, as Pelé held his breath and waited. 'We've been improving every year but now we're dreaming even bigger, and that means unleashing you in the first team.'

Pelé beamed. 'I'm ready!' he said immediately.

'Thanks, Coach!'

'You've earned this chance,' Lula replied, shaking Pelé's hand. 'You put in the hard work and now you're a stronger and more complete player than when you first got here. You're going to have defenders running scared!'

Pelé felt like dancing his way back to the dressing room after that news. Lula clearly had big plans for him this season, and he couldn't wait to play in the Campeonato Paulista.

He learned a lot from his teammates too, particularly Vasconcelos and Del Vecchio who played in a similar position and were always happy to answer questions. The fans were pouring into the Vila Belmiro Stadium these days, wowed by their new Number 10. Pelé got his real Santos debut against AIK, a Sweden club visiting Brazil for a tournament, and showed flashes of his potential with dribbling runs and plenty of tricks.

By now, he was used to being around great players and several who had played for Brazil, but there was still something special about walking next to Pepe on the way out for the warm-up and taking the kick-off with Jair.

'It's like you've been playing for the first team for years!' Del Vecchio said when they walked off the pitch together after the AIK game. 'You were amazing today.'

After the first few months of the season, Pelé was proud of how quickly he had adjusted to playing against some of the best teams in the country. But he knew he could do even more. He had scored a few goals but he wasn't a regular scorer yet, despite all the shooting practice he was doing in training at Vila Belmiro.

Still, he was clearly on the path to becoming a superstar, and his performances earned him a place in a joint Santos/Vasco da Gama squad for a mid-season tournament against top Brazilian and European clubs. Once again, he was sharing a dressing room with the same legends that he had been pretending to be on the playground with Ze Roberto, Vadinho and Ari only a few years before!

The good news kept coming. The Santos/Vasco

team would be playing at the Maracanã Stadium and Pelé just stood and stared when he first walked onto the pitch before the game against Portuguese club Belenenses. The stadium was huge and he felt tiny as he looked up into the highest rows of seats.

In some ways, this match would kickstart the rest of Pelé's season. Inspired by the Maracanã stage, he was everywhere in a 6–1 win. First, the Belenenses defenders made the mistake of letting him control the ball in the penalty area. Pelé quickly created a yard of space and drilled a low shot past the keeper.

Goooooooooooooooooooaaaaaaaaaaaaaaaaallllllllllllll llllllllllll!!!!!!!!!!!!!!!!!!!

But the defenders hadn't learned their lesson. This time, they lunged desperately as Pelé set off on a mazy run, weaving past tackles. He made the last defender look like a statue; he skipped past him and then poked the ball into the net.

Goooooooooooooooooooaaaaaaaaaaaaaaaaallllllllllllll llllllllllll!!!!!!!!!!!!!!!!!!!

Now Pelé's confidence was sky high. 'Lay it back,' he called from just outside the box. The pass came fast, but he didn't even need a touch to control it. He just relied on his instincts and smashed the ball with his right foot. Before anyone could move, the shot arrowed into the top corner.

Goooooooooooooooooooooaaaaaaaaaaaaaaaaalllllllllllllll llllllllllll!!!!!!!!!!!!!!!!!!!!!

He was still celebrating that hat-trick when his run of good news continued. His performances had caught the attention of the Brazil national team coaches and he would be part of the squad for the next game.

Pelé couldn't wait to tell his family his big news, and he could hear the pride (and the tears) straightaway when he spoke to his parents.

'This… this… is one of the happiest days of my life!' was Dondinho's response, stumbling with the words in his excitement. 'Our son is going to be playing for Brazil!'

As with everything else in this whirlwind year, Pelé tried to stay calm and enjoy the experience. He got a warm welcome when he joined the Brazil squad, and he was relieved to see familiar faces like Santos teammate Del Vecchio.

There wasn't much time to be nervous anyway, with two games against Argentina in the Copa Roca coming up. Pelé just focused on showing the Brazil coaches that he was ready to help the team. He was an instant hit in training, as the other players got a closer look at the sixteen-year-old talent they had heard so much about.

Pelé was picked as one of the substitutes for the first leg against Argentina, back at the Maracanã. As he jogged along the touchline, he thought about the goals he had recently scored here for the Santos/Vasco team. He just hoped that Coach Feola would give him a chance to keep his scoring run going.

With Brazil losing 1–0, it was Pelé time! He jogged onto the pitch and quickly started finding space away from the Argentina defence. He had been watching closely from the bench and knew which defenders to target.

Then he saw Tite bursting into the box. He got into position for a cutback pass, but two defenders rushed over to block off the space. Pelé didn't give up on it though. He made another run, getting closer to Tite so it was a simpler pass.

Tite managed to squeeze the ball across and Pelé pounced on the chance, firing a shot past the keeper and two diving defenders.

Goooooooooooooooooooooaaaaaaaaaaaaaaaaalllllllllllllll llllllllllllll!!!!!!!!!!!!!!!!!!!!!

He leapt in the air as his teammates crowded round him. Argentina hit back to win 2–1, but the Pelé buzz was growing ahead of the second leg.

Feola had seen enough in the first leg to pick Pelé in the starting line-up, and he was rewarded within twenty minutes when Brazil went ahead. Picking up a loose ball just outside the box, Pelé only had one thought in his mind – shoot! But he didn't rush it. No one was closing him down so he took two more touches, then curled the ball past the keeper's outstretched hand.

Goooooooooooooooooooooaaaaaaaaaaaaaaaaalllllllllllllll llllllllllllll!!!!!!!!!!!!!!!!!!!!!

That strike set Brazil on their way to winning the Copa Roca and Pelé was in the middle of all the celebrations. He was an international footballer now!

He just hoped he had done enough to earn a regular place in the squad.

Back at Santos, Pelé was flying. Playing as if he had years of experience, he finished as the top scorer in the league. He had quickly become a fan favourite and some of his older teammates enjoyed ducking away from autograph hunters by sending them in Pelé's direction.

Reflecting on an incredible year, Pelé was glad he had kept his kit from his international debut as a reminder of that milestone, and there were plenty more special moments ahead for him in a Brazil shirt.

CHAPTER 12

BRAZIL'S GOLDEN BOY

As the 1958 World Cup got closer and closer, the
dream of playing on that global stage was within
reach for Pelé. Listening on an old radio, he found out
that he had been picked in the Brazil squad despite
an unlucky injury during a warm-up friendly against
Corinthians. A strong tackle had come out of nowhere
as he controlled a pass, leaving Pelé on the floor
holding his knee. He had feared the worst when he
couldn't even walk without limping.

'When will I be able to play again?' he kept asking
the doctor.

But Pelé breathed a big sigh of relief when the
doctor confirmed that it wasn't the type of injury that

would require months of recovery and that he should be fit for some of the group games. The excitement for the tournament was building, with more and more fans and reporters at each training session.

As the Brazil squad boarded the plane to Sweden, Pelé couldn't help but smile. Here he was, sitting on a plane with the best players in the country and preparing for the World Cup. He tried to make the most of the moment, just like everyone kept telling him, but that wasn't easy. This was the dream of just about every teenage boy in Brazil and there were still days when he could hardly believe it was all real.

'Try to get some sleep,' suggested Gilmar, the team's keeper, spotting Pelé's nervous fidgeting on the plane.

Pelé nodded and leaned towards his headrest. He closed his eyes and thought about some of the goals that had led him to this moment.

Once they arrived in Sweden, all Pelé could do was work on exercises and stretches to strengthen his knee. He put all his energy into his recovery, because he was determined to be at his best for the biggest games of his life. He worked hard in each session with the team doctor and did his best to adjust to all the changes in his life – the pressure on the team at a big tournament, the extra security around the hotel, the questions from reporters. Wherever he went, he had a smile on his face.

'Doesn't any of this make you nervous?' Gilmar, the Brazil keeper, asked as Pelé walked back towards the team bus with a grin on his face. He had just finished signing a few autographs and joking with some of the Swedish fans.

He smiled and gave a playful shrug. 'I feel like the luckiest guy alive to be here at the World Cup,' he said. 'What's better than this? I just hope I'll have a chance to show what I can do.'

'As long as you're fit, you'll get a chance, trust me,' Gilmar added. 'There's no one like you, and the coaches know it. You make scoring goals look so easy.'

'Well, even if I'm a bit nervous, the opposition defenders should probably be more nervous,' he said, laughing. 'They've got to deal with me!'

Gilmar laughed too, but he had a feeling that his fearless young teammate was totally serious.

Pelé was relieved to feel less and less pain in his knee as the tournament began, but Brazil still took a careful approach and he didn't play in the first two games. Though it was hard to watch from the bench, he was in a much better mood when he was allowed to rejoin the training sessions.

'I feel good,' he told the coaches after testing his knee in some of the drills. 'It's time to get back to scoring goals again.'

He was ready to make his mark in the rest of the World Cup, and it helped that he was a secret weapon. Opponents knew lots about Vavá, Didi and Garrincha, but not this teenager who was bursting onto the scene.

Pelé was back in the team for Brazil's final group game against the USSR and it felt amazing to finally be back doing what he did best. Two goals from Vavá fired the Brazilians to a 2–0 win that put them top of the group and set up a quarter-final against Wales.

But Wales made life difficult for Brazil, and Pelé was still getting his sharpness back after his weeks of rest. He could see why his coaches kept saying that real games would have a different feel than the training sessions. At half-time, it was still 0–0.

'Time for some magic,' Coach Feola said, looking at his attackers.

Pelé smiled. He had been thinking the same thing. Wales weren't creating chances at the other end, so one goal might be enough to reach the semi-final.

Then it happened. Didi chipped a pass into the box and Pelé controlled the ball on his chest, while holding off his marker. Sensing the defender was now off balance, Pelé took advantage. Wales were expecting him to lay the ball back to a teammate or spin to get the ball onto his right foot. Instead, he went the other way, flicking the ball past the defender, then firing a shot into the bottom corner.

Gooooooooooooooooooooaaaaaaaaaaaaaaaallllllllllllll llllllllllll!!!!!!!!!!!!!!!!!!!

He jumped in the air twice and ended up in the net with the ball as all the players piled on top of him, sensing Pelé's joy and relief.

'It's good to be back!' he said to Didi as they high-fived after the final whistle. Brazil were through to a semi-final against France and still on track for World Cup glory for the first time.

Back to full fitness, everything was clicking for Pelé. In training, he was scoring from all angles and fooling defenders with quick turns or little flicks. In this kind of form, he didn't look like a seventeen-year-old at his first World Cup.

For forty-five minutes, France matched Brazil's pace and movement. The Brazilians led 2–1 at half-time thanks to goals from Vavá and Didi, but there were plenty of nervy moments for their defenders.

In the second half, Pelé took over. His pace was starting to stretch the French defenders and he was getting more space to shoot. First, the France keeper fumbled a cross from the left wing, and Pelé got there first to tap the ball in.

Goooooooooooooooooooaaaaaaaaaaaaaaaaalllllllllllllll llllllllllll!!!!!!!!!!!!!!!!!!!

Then Garrincha swept over a cross from the right wing and Pelé tried a lay-off to Vavá. Instead, a defender blocked it, but the ball rolled back to Pelé, and he whipped a shot into the net with the outside of his boot.

*Goooooooooooooooooooooaaaaaaaaaaaaaaaaalllllllllllllll
lllllllllllllll!!!!!!!!!!!!!!!!!!!!!*

Brazil were leading 4–1. The final was in sight now!

If Brazil were cruising, Pelé wasn't finished yet.
He raced away from his marker again as a long
pass floated through to him. He controlled it on his
thigh and the ball sat up for a volley. Pelé connected
perfectly and his shot flew past the keeper.

*Goooooooooooooooooooooaaaaaaaaaaaaaaaaalllllllllllllll
lllllllllllllll!!!!!!!!!!!!!!!!!!!!!*

A hat-trick in the World Cup semi-final! There
were smiles on all the Brazil faces after that result,
but there was still work to do. They would be taking
on the hosts, Sweden, in the final, and Pelé knew
that Brazil would be entering a stadium packed with
Swedish fans.

'We're just going to have to spoil the big party!'
he said as he took turns with Vavá and Didi in the
shooting drills.

Sweden scored first in the final and suddenly there
were a few doubts. Brazil had never won the World

Cup and none of the players wanted a repeat of the disappointment of the 1950 final. But Pelé didn't panic. There was plenty of time left – and he knew he could get the better of the Sweden defence.

Two goals from Vavá turned the game in Brazil's favour and then Pelé looked like the freshest player on the pitch in the second half.

When Nílton Santos looked up and swept a long ball into the box, Pelé had already drifted towards the back post. As two defenders scrambled backwards, he had the perfect view. He chested the ball down to leave one defender out of position, then with the most delicate of touches, he dinked it over the head of the last defender. The ball floated back down into his path and he thumped a volley into the bottom corner.

Goooooooooooooooooooooaaaaaaaaaaaaaaaalllllllllllllll llllllllllll!!!!!!!!!!!!!!!!!!!

Pelé skipped away to celebrate, with both arms in the air. 3–1.

Now he could see the fear in the faces of the Sweden defenders, and he kept giving them nightmares by dropping short to lay the ball off, running out to the wings or sprinting behind the last defender. Even some of the Sweden fans were buzzing with excitement when Pelé got the ball.

Mário Zagallo made it 4–1, Sweden pulled a goal back and then Pelé had the final word.

In the last minute, he back-heeled the ball to Zagallo on the left wing and then raced into the box with his arm up, calling for a cross. Zagallo chipped the ball across and Pelé arrived just in time to head the ball over the keeper and into the net.

Goooooooooooooooooooooaaaaaaaaaaaaaaaaalllllllllllllll lllllllllllll!!!!!!!!!!!!!!!!!!!

Within seconds of the final whistle, the achievement sunk in for Pelé. He thought about his family listening to the game at home and all the parties across Brazil. The moment washed over him in a wave of emotion – joy and pride, relief and exhaustion. Suddenly he was crying on Gilmar's shoulder and he couldn't stop.

Pelé just about had time to dry his eyes before the trophy presentation. He followed his teammates up the steps as captain Hilderaldo Bellini picked up the trophy and raised it to the sky.

It was all a blur for Pelé, but he snapped back into the present when the World Cup trophy made its way along the line of Brazil players and eventually reached him. For a second, he just stared at it with a big smile spreading across his face. Was this really happening?!

What a day! It was the World Cup glory that Brazil had been waiting for – and the trophy that he had promised Dondinho just eight years ago. Pelé joined in the lap of honour around the stadium and the singing and dancing in the dressing room. Most of all, though, he couldn't wait to speak to his family and hear about the party going on back home.

CHAPTER 13

BROKEN RECORDS AND BEAUTIFUL GOALS

Returning from the 1958 World Cup as a champion and key goalscorer, Pelé wanted to use those achievements as a launch pad for his season at Santos. Sure, the parade and the parties with his Brazil teammates had been great fun, but he didn't let the success go to his head.

From the minute he put on the Santos shirt that year, he was an unstoppable goal machine. Still playing alongside Pepe and now also stars like Pagão, Coutinho and Dorval, Pelé had never had so many scoring chances – and he took full advantage of them.

Four goals against XV de Novembro, then four more against Nacional.

Five goals against Ypiranga, then another four against Comercial.

Four goals again to beat both Corinthians and Guarani.

Pelé was making it all look ridiculously easy. Even in his quieter games, he was still scoring hat-tricks. Suddenly it was normal for Santos to win 8–0 or 9–1.

Before a game against Botafogo, Feola was preparing to give his players some final instructions.

'Okay, let's go over the tactics for today,' he said. 'I want to make sure you all know what your jobs are.'

'Get the ball to Pelé?' Coutinho suggested, making everyone laugh.

'Well, yes, that plan seems to be working pretty well for us!' Feola replied. 'But don't just rely on Pelé. Let's get forward to support him.'

Sure enough, Pelé scored a hat-trick and Santos won 4–0.

If anyone thought Santos's dominant start was a fluke, those doubts didn't last long. The team was unbeatable and went on to win the Campeonato Paulista. As Pelé lifted his first trophy with Santos, he waved to the fans. He was glad that the club was turning down offers from top European clubs and he wanted to build on this special year. He could barely believe that he finished the season with a tally of fifty-eight goals.

'My teammates do a great job of setting me up,' Pelé was always quick to say. That was true, but there were also many goals that he created out of nothing.

Up against three defenders or seemingly trapped near the corner, he just dipped into his bag of tricks. Seconds later, he had escaped, and there was usually only one outcome when he got within shooting distance.

Expectations were even higher heading into the 1959 season, but life became more difficult for Pelé, who had begun his required year of service in the army. That meant he was doing exercises, cleaning and other chores as part of his soldier duties as well as training and playing for Santos.

Before long, he was also playing for his division of the army as well as the overall army team. If he was lucky, he would get a day off in between games.

His love of football and his brilliance on the pitch got him through it, but his body paid a price with so many games.

Eventually, he worked out that he had played over 100 matches across the different teams in 1959. Santos fell short of defending the Campeonato Paulista title that year, but they did win the Torneio Rio-São Paulo.

'I never thought I'd say that I was playing too much football, but that's how I feel this year,' he told his Santos teammates as he limped back to the dressing room after their latest win.

Though the aches and pains were still there, Pelé could finally return to more rest days for the 1960 season, and it made a difference as Santos won the Campeonato Paulista. He scored forty-seven goals, including hat-tricks against Jabaquara and Noroeste.

The highlights kept coming. Pelé always loved playing at the Maracanã Stadium, and he had a good feeling when he stepped onto the pitch to face Fluminense there during the 1961 season. When he was little, Pelé had loved the idea of becoming a pilot, and he sometimes had that flying sensation during his gliding, weaving runs. That day at the Maracanã, he picked up the ball near his own penalty area, turned and saw that he had space to start dribbling.

The Fluminense players sensed the danger and two midfielders ran over. But they were too late. Pelé was into his stride now – he went inside and outside, right foot then left foot, swaying but never falling. Another Fluminense player lunged in but Pelé easily dribbled around the outstretched leg.

Now he was passing the halfway line, and he could see Fluminense players rushing from all directions while others scrambled backwards. It was a full-scale panic! Pelé found an extra gear, moving even faster and leaving two more defenders on the ground.

He looked up at the edge of the box and saw the last few defenders charging at him. Pelé was running so fast that it only took a small drop of the shoulder to dodge the first tackle, then another fake to beat the last two. Before the keeper could even dive, Pelé fired the ball into the net.

Goooooooooooaaaaaaaaallllllllllllllllllll!!!!!!!!!!!!

Turning around to celebrate, he counted seven Fluminense players on the floor. He had almost dribbled the entire length of the pitch, and no one could stop him.

'Not bad, right?' Pelé said as Pepe and Dorval ran over to him with total shock on their faces.

'Are you even human?!' Dorval asked, grinning and putting his arm round Pelé.

It would become known as the Gol de Placa, with a special bronze plaque put up at the Maracanã.

CHAPTER 14

CHEERING ON THE CHAMPS

After all his Santos heroics, it was time for Pelé
to focus on the national team again. As the 1962
World Cup kicked off, there were sixteen teams and
hundreds of players in Chile for the tournament, but
most of the excitement was focused on one man –
Pelé. This was set up to be his tournament, as the
world's best player and the type of magician on the
ball that the crowds were desperate to see.

Pelé knew that he had played a lot of games over
the past few years, but there was no time to worry
about his sore body. He was sure that most players
were dealing with some sort of small injury after
a long season. This was the World Cup and the

tournament had become really special for him since his heroic performances in 1958. Now Brazil had to defend the trophy.

Pelé's tournament got off to a good start against Mexico. He got the ball on the right wing and skipped inside away from a tackle. He was strong enough to hold off the next defender and squeeze his way into the box. Another Mexico player tried to pull his shirt, but Pelé was too quick. He brushed that off, lined up a shot with his left foot and swept the ball into the bottom corner.

Gooooooooooooooooooooaaaaaaaaaaaaaaaallllllllllllll llllllllllll!!!!!!!!!!!!!!!!!!!

Pelé was shining brightly for Brazil at the World Cup again, but in the next game against Czechoslovakia, disaster struck. As he stretched to dribble between two players, he felt a sharp pain in his leg. He ended up on the ground and he stayed there as the team doctor came to check on him.

He hobbled over to the touchline and knew there was no way that he could go back on. Brazil made a substitution and Pelé's thoughts shifted to whether he would be fit for any of the rest of the tournament.

The signs weren't good. He started treatment but it was likely that the injury would need at least a few weeks to heal.

Rather than sulking or flying home, Pelé instead focused on being the best possible teammate. He still turned up for training, clapping and encouraging. He spoke up if he spotted something and did his best to ease the pressure on Amarildo, his replacement.

When Amarildo scored two goals against Spain in the last group game, Pelé was the first to congratulate him. He knew what it was like to be thrown into a World Cup with big expectations.

'Keep making those runs because Garrincha and Vavá are always looking for the pass,' Pelé said. 'You're doing a great job.'

As he went through all the exercises recommended by the doctor, Pelé refused to give up hope of recovering in time for the World Cup final, if Brazil made it that far. Deep down, though, he knew it would take a miracle for him to be fit.

He tried some gentle jogging and short passes. Some

days, he felt more positive about his chances. Other days, the pain left him fearing the worst. But he tried to stay upbeat for his teammates, who were dealing with their own nerves and challenges.

With wins over England and Chile, the Brazilians powered on and reached the final, which would be a rematch against Czechoslovakia.

'Let me give it a proper test at training tomorrow,' Pelé said to the Brazil coaches. 'My leg has felt better over the last two days.'

The coaches agreed to do a fitness test in training. They knew how much it meant to Pelé and how hard he had worked to give himself a chance.

But within minutes, Pelé was on the floor, waving his arm to signal that he needed some help. He had just hit his first long pass and he instantly felt the intense muscle pain. Pelé knew what that meant. His dream of returning for the final was over.

Back in his hotel room, Pelé burst into tears. It all seemed so unfair.

'I can't believe this is happening,' he told the team doctor. 'Why now? Why in a World Cup? These are the games that I live for!'

Brazil didn't rule him out, just to keep Czechoslovakia guessing, but his only job now was to help his teammates get ready for one of the biggest games of their lives. Despite going 1–0 down in the final, the Brazilians powered back for a 3–1 win, with Amarildo, Zito and Vavá scoring the goals.

Brazil had done it again. Two World Cups in a row. It wasn't how Pelé had pictured the tournament, but he was thrilled for his teammates.

The rest of the world would have four years to try to catch up, but Pelé already had his sights set on dominating that next World Cup.

CHAPTER 15

A COPA CROWN

Returning to Brazil as back-to-back World Cup winners was an amazing feeling. Pelé saw smiling faces, banners, food baskets and many other different ways to mark the occasion. Sure, he wished that he had been able to play a bigger role in defending the trophy, but it was impossible not to get swept away by all the excitement and energy in the crowds swarming the streets.

Now it was back to business with Santos. Pelé had powered the club to São Paulo's Campeonato Paulista three times along with the national Brasileiro title in 1961 – and the Copa Libertadores was next on his list. The Copa Libertadores featured the best clubs in

South America and this year Santos had qualified.

'This is the big one,' Pelé told his teammates. 'We'll be legends if we bring home the Copa Libertadores.'

Prior to the World Cup break, Santos had cruised through the group stage. But as the semi-finals began, Pelé was still recovering from his injury. It was taking much longer than he had expected, and it would keep him out of the semi-final.

After the World Cup heartbreak, this was a cruel blow. All Pelé wanted to do was get on the pitch and help his teammates. But Santos battled on without him and beat Universidad Católica thanks to goals from Lima and Zito.

Now Uruguay's Peñarol, winners of the last two Copa Libertadores, were waiting for Santos in the final. It was the type of stage that Pelé loved, but until he could run and kick the ball like normal, there was nothing he could do.

'Be patient with yourself,' Lula urged him. 'Your body will tell you when you're ready to come back. If you try to rush it, you could be out for even longer.'

Pelé knew Lula was right. He had heard stories

of players rushing back too soon and making their injuries much worse. But it was still a crushing blow to be a spectator once again.

In his absence, Santos stunned Peñarol in the first leg, winning 2–1 in Uruguay, but Peñarol hit back in the second leg and won 3–2. The scores were tied 4–4 on aggregate.

Now there would be a playoff, and *finally, finally, finally*, Pelé was back. His return boosted the whole squad as they travelled to Argentina for a one-game play-off on a neutral field.

Pelé was relieved but restless to get back on the pitch. It had been so hard to watch all the huge games and not be able to play his part, but now his leg felt much better. He just hoped he wouldn't be too rusty after such a long break.

Sensing his star striker's frustration after missing so many big games lately, Lula called Pelé over during the warm-up.

'Don't put too much pressure on yourself,' Lula said, patting Pelé on the shoulder. 'Settle into the game at your own pace, and your moment will come,

I know it. We're all going to see some of that Pelé magic tonight.'

Santos looked like a different team with Pelé flying forward and taking on defenders, and they got an early lead after a Peñarol own goal. The ball was fizzing around the pitch again, and Santos were turning defence into attack in an instant.

But Pelé was still hungry for a goal. Early in the second half, he saw Dorval burst forward on the right wing, knocking the ball past his marker. Pelé darted towards the penalty area, then hung back just outside the box. Dorval floated a cross towards him, but it went too far and landed at Coutinho's feet.

Coutinho shuffled a pass to Pelé, who controlled it instantly between three Peñarol defenders. There wasn't much room to work with, but Pelé knew what he wanted to do. He just shifted the ball slightly to make space for a shot and then smashed a screamer into the top corner.

Gooooooooooooooooooooaaaaaaaaaaaaaaaaalllllllllllllll llllllllllllll!!!!!!!!!!!!!!!!!!!!

It was a breathtaking strike, and Pelé punched the

air. It felt like he had been waiting a long time for that moment.

'The King is back!' his teammates yelled, jumping on his back.

Tired legs in the Peñarol defence gave him another chance in the final minutes. None of the defenders could clear the ball and Pelé pounced to whip a quick shot through a crowd of bodies.

Goooooooooooooooooooooaaaaaaaaaaaaaaaaaalllllllllllllll llllllllllll!!!!!!!!!!!!!!!!!!!

It was the dream ending to a dream night for Pelé, and the Santos players rushed to him at the final whistle. They had become the first Brazilian team to win the Copa Libertadores and their star man had proved once again that he was the best player in the world.

Riding the joy of winning the Copa Libertadores, Pelé continued his unstoppable form in the Campeonato Paulista. He raced to thirty-seven goals as Santos also clinched the Brasileiro title again to add to a trophy cabinet that was at risk of overflowing.

CHAPTER 16

THE
INTERCONTINENTAL ICON

'Back to the Maracanã!' Pelé shouted, climbing onto the team bus.

The big games kept coming for Pelé and Santos. As the 1962 Copa Libertadores champions, they would now compete for the Intercontinental Cup in a two-legged tie against Portuguese giants Benfica.

The first leg was set for the Maracanã Stadium, which held far more people than Santos's usual home at Vila Belmiro, and there was lots of excitement for this battle of global stars. Pelé stood on one side of the halfway line in his Number 10 shirt; Benfica's Eusébio stood across from him in his Number 9 shirt.

Pelé had shown South American crowds that he was

back in top form in the Copa Libertadores play-off, and this was an opportunity to send that same message to a European audience. He had great memories at the Maracanã and he seemed to hit every shot sweetly in the warm-up. As Gilmar picked the ball out of the net for what felt like the fiftieth time, he laughed and gave Pelé a look that suggested he might like some shots that he had a chance of saving.

Once the game started, it didn't take long for Pelé to make his mark. A looping cross pinballed around in the box and he was always alert to that kind of chance. When the ball bounced loose again, he reacted first to bundle it into the net.

Gooooooooooooooooooooaaaaaaaaaaaaaaaaaalllllllllllllll llllllllllll!!!!!!!!!!!!!!!!!!!

It was one of the ugliest goals that Pelé could remember scoring, but he didn't mind.

'I thought you only scored beautiful goals,' Pepe teased. 'You're human after all!'

Benfica fought back to make it 1–1, then Coutinho put Santos ahead again. With just five minutes left, Pelé was still on the hunt for chances, and a promising attack sent Pepe through on goal. His shot was well saved, but the ball rebounded right to Pelé's left foot. Without even thinking, he thumped a low strike into the bottom corner.

Goooooooooooooooooooooaaaaaaaaaaaaaaaaalllllllllllllll lllllllllllll!!!!!!!!!!!!!!!!!!!!!

He had only just finished celebrating when Benfica scored an even later goal. After the game, there was a sense that the 3–2 scoreline made the Portuguese club favourites heading into the second leg. But Pelé disagreed.

'I think we're in a great position,' he told Pepe and Coutinho back in the dressing room. 'Benfica will probably push forward more in their own stadium and that's when we'll pounce.'

Pelé had to wait almost a month for the trip to Lisbon for the second leg, but he had a good feeling as soon as he stepped off the bus at the Estádio da Luz. He loved these big games and he was in great goalscoring form.

With the whole world tuning in again for the Pelé vs Eusébio showdown, Santos took control in the first half. Pepe set off on a run down the left and Pelé sprinted to get into the box. He knew Pepe liked to whip in early crosses and, sure enough, the ball fizzed across from the left wing. The pitch was slippery but Pelé reacted just in time to slide forward and steer the ball into the net.

Goooooooooooooooooooaaaaaaaaaaaaaaaalllllllllllll llllllllllll!!!!!!!!!!!!!!!!!!!

That great start soon got even better. Pelé picked up a pass thirty yards out and danced away from one defender with a dip of his shoulder. Now he was dribbling faster and faster. A tackle flew in but he swayed to his left and managed to keep his balance. With the ball on his left foot, he raced into the box and thumped a low shot past the goalkeeper's dive and into the bottom corner.

Goooooooooooooooooooaaaaaaaaaaaaaaaalllllllllllll llllllllllll!!!!!!!!!!!!!!!!!!!

The Benfica fans went silent. Their team had no answer to Pelé's wizardry. After half-time, he conjured up another goal – this time it was a run down the right that drew three defenders towards him and then a perfect cross for Coutinho to score the simplest tap-in.

'Whoa, it's like you're playing a different sport!' Coutinho called out as he rushed over to hug Pelé. 'I almost forgot to run forward because I was too busy watching you!'

'I'm just making up for lost time!' Pelé replied. Thankfully, his injury was becoming a distant memory.

The Benfica defenders were backing off every time Pelé got the ball, and he used that to his advantage with another lightning move. He burst past the last defender, saw the keeper save his first attempt and sprinted on to poke the rebound into the net.

Goooooooooooooooooooaaaaaaaaaaaaaaaaalllllllllllll llllllllllll!!!!!!!!!!!!!!!!!!!

An Intercontinental Cup hat-trick! The game finished 5–2, but it wasn't even that close. Pelé and Santos were on another level.

Pelé joined his teammates to collect yet another trophy. Despite the World Cup injury that had seemed to last forever, it had turned out to be a very good year.

'That might be the best game I've ever seen you play,' Pepe said as they held the Intercontinental Cup in the air together. 'Benfica are a great team and you destroyed them.'

Pelé grinned. Pepe was right. There weren't many other games that had given him this kind of joy. In a matchup of two star-studded teams, Pelé had shone brightest.

'I arrived hoping to stop a great man,' the Benfica goalkeeper later explained, 'but I went away convinced that I had been undone by a man not born on the same planet as the rest of us.'

That just about summed up Pelé's otherworldly performance.

CHAPTER 17

ON THE TROPHY HUNT AGAIN

'Quick, in here!' Pelé said, while he and a few friends attempted to hide from a group of cameramen. 'I can't even get back to my house now without people wanting to take photos for the newspapers.'

Heading into the 1963 season, 'Pelé mania' had reached another level. Crowds followed him everywhere he went – and on the pitch, he was becoming an even bigger nightmare for defenders.

Though Santos fell short of defending the Campeonato Paulista, Pelé knew that repeating as Copa Libertadores champions would still make this a memorable season. After playing so many games over the past few years, he was relieved that Santos, as the

1962 winners, got a free pass through to the semi-finals, where they would face Botafogo.

Pelé grinned when he saw that matchup. He knew this Botafogo team well, with Brazil teammates Garrincha and Jairzinho leading the attack.

'That's a great team over there,' Pelé said to Coutinho and Lima as they passed the ball around in a little circle. 'But we're a great team too and we'll prove that over these two games.'

Pelé's last-minute equaliser saved Santos from a loss at home in the first leg, but they had a tough task ahead of them when they travelled to Rio de Janeiro for the second leg.

But the Santos dressing room was always full of confidence. They had Pelé and no one else did.

'Find a way to win,' Lula urged his players in the dressing room. 'It doesn't have to be pretty, but let's start on the front foot and get that first goal. Make them feel the pressure.'

And that's exactly what Pelé did. In a game featuring many Brazil greats, Pelé delivered a superstar performance. He ripped through the Botafogo defence for a stunning first-half hat-trick, scoring with a clinical chip, a leaping header and a well-placed penalty.

There was a huge crowd packed into the Maracanã Stadium, but Pelé had silenced them all. Santos wrapped up a 4–0 win and now only Boca Juniors stood between them and a second straight Copa Libertadores trophy.

This time, Santos would be playing the first leg at home and they carried on where they left off against Botafogo. Two goals for Coutinho and another for Lima made it 3–0 before half-time. But Santos lost focus and Boca hit back to cut the score to 3–2.

'Boca were on the ropes and we let them back in,' Lula said, pacing around the dressing room. 'We're going to need to be at our best in the second leg because that Boca stadium is going to be rocking.'

Pelé agreed, but he was looking at the positives. Santos still had a lead to take to Argentina and there was plenty of experience in their team. Pelé, Pepe and Coutinho had played together in so many big games. They could handle a noisy crowd.

But that was really put to the test when Boca took

the lead. The home fans were screaming, cheering and yelling insults at the Santos players. Pelé looked over at Pepe and Coutinho and gave them a nod that said 'it's time to take over'.

They didn't have to wait long for a chance. A poor Boca clearance only went as far as Dorval, and he flicked the ball straight to Pelé. Pelé took the pass down on his chest, took another touch to draw the defenders towards him, then slipped the ball through to Coutinho, who thumped in the equaliser.

'That's more like it!' Pelé shouted to his teammates. The Boca fans stopped singing so loudly.

Now the tackles were flying in, and Pelé got the worst of the fouls. But he kept his cool and just bounced up to get on with the game.

Boca were running out of time and throwing more players forward. That meant lots of space for the Santos front three. With ten minutes left, Pelé dribbled towards the edge of the box. A defender went in for the tackle but the ball rebounded right back to Pelé. If that touch was a little fortunate, there was nothing lucky about his shot. It arrowed into the bottom corner, leaving the keeper on the ground.

Gooooooooooooooooooooaaaaaaaaaaaaaaaaallllllllllllll llllllllllll!!!!!!!!!!!!!!!!!!!!!

'Yes!!!' Pelé screamed, jumping and punching the air again and again. That one really felt good. He turned to celebrate in front of the Boca fans and saw some of them heading for the stadium exit. Game over!

When Pelé walked around the dressing room to hug each of his teammates, he was tired but incredibly happy. He knew better than most people how hard it was to win these big trophies. Nothing came easily and it took great teamwork, talent and a little slice of luck to end up as champions.

The next few years confirmed how difficult it was to keep winning. Santos were eliminated in the Copa Libertadores semi-finals in 1964 and 1965, but they continued their dominance in the Campeonato Paulista and the Brasileiro.

Pelé was still in his mid-twenties, but his body had been through more football games than anyone else his age. Luckily, Santos had hired Professor

Mazzei to take a closer look at all aspects of the club's preparation, from training through to match days. Mazzei had plenty of new ideas, and Pelé was soon feeling fresher than he had in a long time.

With another World Cup coming up, that was good news for all Brazil fans.

CHAPTER 18

BLOODIED AND BRUISED

Pelé couldn't wait to be back on the big stage at the 1966 World Cup. Brazil were going for a hat-trick of World Cup trophies, and he was arriving in good scoring form.

But there were some worrying signs as the Brazil squad arrived in England for the tournament. Though Pelé knew this was going to be their biggest test yet, he sensed some overconfidence and disorganisation as they were preparing for their first game. While the players were focused on the job ahead, Pelé couldn't understand some of the decisions being made by Brazil's Technical Commission, which was in charge of all the planning and team selection.

'Teams are going to be desperate to beat us,' he told some of his newer teammates. 'We can't afford a slow start.'

'Exactly – and if teams can't beat us with skill, they're going to push and pull and kick,' Garrincha added.

Pelé knew that Brazil would have to prove they could win the ugly games when their beautiful football wasn't working. Talent alone wouldn't be enough, and it didn't take long for Pelé to see that physical play would often go unpunished by the referees.

Brazil started the tournament against Bulgaria, and Pelé got off to a fast start. He was tripped on the edge of the box and he quickly grabbed the ball to take the free kick. As he waited for the referee's whistle, Pelé spotted a gap to the side of the Bulgaria wall, with the keeper a few steps too far to the right. That's where he aimed, hitting a hard low shot that skidded into the net.

Goooooooooooooooooooaaaaaaaaaaaaaaaallllllllllllll llllllllllll!!!!!!!!!!!!!!!!!

But then the kicks and trips started to get worse,

leaving Pelé and the other Brazil attackers with nasty cuts and bruises. Brazil won 2–0 and Pelé got through the ninety minutes, but he needed bags of ice back in the dressing room.

The pain was much worse the next day and suddenly he was getting flashbacks to the 1962 tournament and all his treatment sessions.

'I'll be fine,' he reassured the coaches. 'This is the World Cup, and it'll take more than a few kicks to keep me out.'

But with Pelé hobbling around the training pitch, the Technical Commission stepped in and decided that he should be rested for the next group game. That was the last thing Pelé wanted to hear, but he trusted his teammates to battle on without him.

The plan backfired spectacularly, though. Hungary scored after two minutes and went on to beat Brazil 3–1. Pelé had his head in his hands on the bench, feeling completely helpless. What a mess!

Back at the hotel that night, Pelé couldn't sleep. 'I should have been out there,' he kept muttering to himself as walked around his room. This was supposed to be his big World Cup comeback after the injury heartbreak in 1962, but now he was worried about the team being knocked out at the first hurdle.

Suddenly, Brazil were in trouble in the group table. Other results meant that they would need to win their last game against Portugal to qualify for the knockout rounds, and that just added more pressure to a squad that was already on edge.

Though Pelé was back in the starting line-up for this decisive match, it was a nightmare from start to finish. With other players also being pulled in and out of the team, there was confusion everywhere – and Portugal took advantage.

In truth, Pelé never had a chance to impact the game. Any time he controlled the ball, he instantly felt a kick in his shin or a push in the back. One bad tackle sent him tumbling to the floor. It was a clear foul, but there was no whistle.

'Ouch!' he yelled, as he grabbed his knee and looked in amazement at the referee. 'Ref, how is that not a free kick?!'

Then another trip stopped him from setting off on

a run, and a hard shove blocked him from chasing a through ball. It didn't even feel like a football game anymore.

Portugal were 2–0 up at half-time and Eusébio later put the finishing touches on the win with his second goal. After the game, Pelé walked slowly off the pitch. Everything hurt – his back, his legs, his feet. He could feel blood trickling down his shins from a few different cuts on his knees. Brazil were out, and this was a horrible way to end a miserable tournament.

As Pelé walked down the tunnel that night, limping and close to tears, he really wasn't sure that he ever wanted to play at the World Cup again.

CHAPTER 19

O MILÉSIMO!

Pelé put the disappointment of the 1966 World Cup
behind him by doing the only thing he could think
of – winning more trophies. He powered Santos to the
Campeonato Paulista in 1967, 1968 and 1969, with
his usual mix of breathtaking goals and inch-perfect
assists. He even added the Intercontinental Supercup
and another Brasileiro title in 1968 too.

But no matter what he did in Santos games, Pelé
kept getting the same question from reporters and fans
– was he really serious about never wearing the Brazil
shirt again?

'I'm just focused on Santos at the moment,' he
explained each time. There was always another

trophy to chase, and he still had the scars from the last World Cup.

But Pelé soon realised that a third straight Campeonato Paulista title wasn't the only major milestone within reach that year. He discovered he only needed a few more goals to get to 1,000 in his career. When he first heard about this, he was stunned.

'Seriously?' he asked the Santos staff. 'That's incredible!'

He had stopped counting his goals a long time ago, but thankfully someone out there was still keeping track of them. So the countdown was on! He had reached 999 goals as Santos travelled to Rio de Janeiro in November 1969 to take on Vasco da Gama.

'Honestly, it's still hard to believe,' Pelé told Zoca and Maria Lucia. 'When I first started, I just thought it was incredible to get to play the game I love as my job. That was more than enough for me. Now, I'm one away from 1,000 career goals. Not bad for a kid who learned football without any shoes!'

'I guess it's fair to say you've come a long way since

those Sete de Setembro days!' Zoca added, laughing.

O Milésimo, as they called the 1,000th goal in Brazil, was the moment that everyone wanted to see. Fans queued for hours for tickets to be able to say they were there for Pelé's special achievement. There was a nervous energy in the Maracanã Stadium that day and Pelé could feel the buzz of the crowd every time he touched the ball near the penalty area. How would they react if he didn't score?

But they all had to be patient. Pelé didn't get a scoring chance in the first half and the fans took a deep breath during the half-time break.

In the second half, Pelé came to life with a quick run, escaping his marker and darting into the box. Another defender rushed over but he was a second too late. His lunging tackle caught Pelé's ankle and they both fell to the floor. Penalty!

Santos's usual penalty-taker Rildo jogged over and scooped up the ball. But before he could put it down on the spot, captain Carlos Alberto rushed into the box, signalling for Pelé to take the penalty instead.

Rildo threw the ball to his teammate and wished

him luck. 'This is it!' Rildo said, with a wink.

Pelé grinned and placed the ball on the penalty spot. He focused on the goal and decided where he was going to aim his shot. After some screams of excitement when the penalty was given, there was now total silence.

Pelé waited for the whistle, then started his run-up. He placed the penalty low to the keeper's left and watched with a mixture of joy and relief as the ball flew into the net.

Gooooooooooooooooooooaaaaaaaaaaaaaaaaalllllllllllllll lllllllllllll!!!!!!!!!!!!!!!!!!!!

'That's O Milésimo – the 1,000th goal for Pelé!' the announcer yelled.

Pelé ran to get the ball and kissed it while still standing in the net. The whole stadium was cheering and clapping. When he turned around to celebrate with his teammates, he saw people everywhere. Photographers and fans were on the pitch. He was lifted into the air and carried on a mini victory lap.

The whole Santos team sprinted over to join in the celebrations. Some of Pelé's teammates had been with him for many those goals, and he knew he owed them a lot for their support and friendship over the years.

'It's been an honour to share the pitch with you, King,' Carlos Alberto said.

'But couldn't you have passed a few of them to me?' Pepe joked.

Pelé just grinned. His head was spinning, and 1,000 goals still sounded unbelievable to him. The game finally continued, though Pelé was still in dreamland. At the end, he remembered to grab the ball so he could keep it as a souvenir from his milestone goal.

Even though the crowd was mostly full of Vasco fans, they all gave Pelé a standing ovation.

To cap off another special season, Santos went on to win the Campeonato Paulista for a third year in a row. The feeling of lifting a trophy and celebrating with his teammates would never get old, no matter how many he won.

While Pelé made the most of a few weeks away from football over the summer, he still felt fresh enough to keep winning.

CHAPTER 20

ON TOP OF THE WORLD AGAIN

Wearing the Brazil shirt for so many years had filled Pelé with incredible pride. He loved his country and so it had been a difficult adjustment when he stepped away from the international stage.

It was even more difficult to see Brazilians going through hard times, with violence and fear becoming more common. The people needed something to bring them together and forget their troubles. With all of this going on, it was no big surprise that the calls for Pelé to boost morale and return to the Brazil team were growing louder and louder.

'The 1970 World Cup is just months away and we need Pelé.'

'He's the greatest player the world has ever seen, and we'll win the tournament if he plays.'

'His Brazil career can't end with that horrible 1966 World Cup.'

Pelé heard it all. He gave it a lot of thought, discussed his options with friends and family, and eventually agreed to rejoin the Brazil squad in the build-up to the 1970 tournament.

But that was only the beginning of the drama. Pelé's relationship with manager João Saldanha was tense and difficult – and when Saldanha was sacked, it was Mario Zagallo, his teammate from the 1958 and 1962 World Cups, who stepped in.

Zagallo didn't have much time before the tournament or a lot of managerial experience. What he did have was Pelé. That meant Brazil had a chance.

However, by the time the World Cup kicked off, it had become popular for reporters and TV shows to question whether Pelé had any of his old magic left. So much had changed since he burst onto the international scene in the 1958 World Cup, and many people remembered the sight of Pelé limping off in the last two World Cups.

No one really knew what to expect from Brazil at the tournament – including the Brazilians themselves. When they went 1–0 down to Czechoslovakia eleven minutes into their first game, it would have been easy for doubts to creep in. But staring at another World Cup setback, Pelé refused to let it happen. He had always embraced these challenges, raising his game when the moment called for it.

Maybe that Czechoslovakia goal was just what Pelé needed to snap him into action. Suddenly he was dribbling with confidence, gliding past defenders and charging towards the goal. No one could get near him.

Rivellino equalised before half-time, Pelé put Brazil ahead in the second half and Jairzinho added two more goals for a 4–1 win.

'Never count us out!' Pelé yelled while his teammates wrapped him in hugs. 'We've still got the champion spirit.'

That win sparked everything for Brazil. They had their swagger back and went on to beat England and Romania in their group. A 4–2 victory over Peru, with Pelé setting up the third goal for Tostão, sent the Brazilians into the semi-finals. But that meant another showdown with Uruguay, who were always such a tough team to play.

'They'll respect us but they won't fear us,' Pelé told his teammates as they sat around the hotel pool. 'We've got to be at our best.'

Despite that warning, Brazil fell behind with a poor first-half performance. There were sloppy passes and silly mistakes as the semi-final pressure kicked in.

'Stay calm,' he called to Rivellino and Jairzinho. 'There's a long way to go.'

Pelé dropped deeper to get on the ball and help settle the team down. Clodoaldo's goal after a quick move down the left made it 1–1 just before the half-time whistle.

Pelé wiped sweat from his forehead when he walked off the pitch with his teammates at half-time. He looked over at Rivellino and puffed out his cheeks. 'We're lucky to still be in this game, but we've got a real chance now,' he said.

At the start of the second half, he could see

that the team needed him to present a classic Pelé performance, and he was at his all-time best in the second half, running at defenders, twisting and turning, and somehow always picking the right pass.

During one run, he got the ball on the halfway line and raced forward, jinking in and out all the way to the edge of the Uruguay box before a defender hacked him down. His confidence was spreading to the rest of the team now too. Then Pelé's little flick sent Tostão into space and he sent a pass through to the sprinting Jairzinho, who outpaced his marker and poked a shot into the net: 2–1.

Pelé leapt in the air and raced over to the touchline to celebrate with Jairzinho and Tostão. He was so fired up now, and he was even more determined to win after the latest crunching foul from the Uruguay defence.

When Brazil stole the ball in midfield, Pelé sensed a chance to finish the game off. He broke away on the left, forcing defenders to scramble back. When they closed in on him, Pelé laid the ball back to Rivellino, who hit a quick shot that crept under the keeper's dive: 3–1.

Another through ball sent Pelé behind the defence again and this time he spotted the keeper running off his line towards him. With an outrageous dummy, Pelé let the ball run past the keeper and skipped round to get to it first, but his shot went just wide.

'That would have been the goal of the tournament!' Jairzinho shouted, with a stunned look on his face.

There would be no Uruguay comeback, and Brazil were into the final. Pelé was so close to delivering the perfect ending to his Brazil career and the kind of joy that the people back home desperately needed. The final against Italy was just days away, but it felt like weeks to Pelé.

He would always remember that bus journey to the Azteca Stadium on the day of the final. Looking out of the window, he saw Brazil flags and a sea of yellow and green. As he waved, the crowd immediately began chanting: 'Pelé! Pelé! Pelé!'

Feeling the love from the fans and the sadness of playing in his last World Cup game, tears trickled down Pelé's cheeks. In a way, he was glad to be dealing with this now so that he could be fully focused when he stepped onto the pitch.

One of the more enjoyable parts of this World Cup journey had been the fun, relaxed mood in the Brazil squad. They had all played a part in getting the team to the final, but Pelé knew that he had to provide the inspiration today. He was the best player and the one who had played in a World Cup final before. He couldn't let his teammates down when they were so close to the big prize.

The stadium was rocking as he followed his teammates down the tunnel and out onto the pitch. Brazil were in their yellow shirts, blue shorts and white socks, with Italy in blue shirts, white shorts and blue socks. Pelé, as always, was wearing the Number 10 shirt – and he had felt tears in his eyes again when he stood in the dressing room and looked down at that shirt, which would always be part of his story.

He knew that fighting back against Uruguay had been a draining test, and he made sure that Brazil got off to a better start in the final. He had some early touches as the Brazilians moved the ball patiently from one side of the pitch to the other, then he ran into the box as Rivellino swept in a looping cross.

Pelé judged it better than the defenders and jumped highest at the back post to head the ball into the bottom corner.

Gooooooooooooooooooooaaaaaaaaaaaaaaaalllllllllllll llllllllllll!!!!!!!!!!!!!!!!!!!!

The emotions poured out of him again. He put his arms up as Jairzinho lifted him into the air. Twelve years on from his first World Cup, he had scored in the final again.

Italy pulled level before half-time and put the pressure back on Brazil, but Pelé still felt confident. After some nail-biting moments at both ends of the pitch, Gérson hit a thunderbolt into the top corner to put the Brazilians ahead again.

Now Italy had to chase another equaliser, and that left them vulnerable to Pelé's magic. First, his cushioned header put the ball right on Jairzinho's foot to make it 3–1. Then it was Pelé's pass that set up Carlos Alberto for a fourth Brazil goal.

When the referee blew the final whistle, everything

was a blur for Pelé. He was surrounded by a huge crowd of people, as teammates, Italy players, fans and reporters rushed to celebrate his third and final time as a World Cup champion.

Then Pelé felt his feet leave the ground as he was carried on the shoulders of his teammates. The Brazil fans got louder and louder in the Azteca Stadium, with flags waving and drums beating. After Carlos Alberto lifted the World Cup trophy high into the air, Pelé got his turn. That trophy meant everything to him. His journey had been bumpy at times, but he was back on top of the world.

'I'm still here!' Pelé shouted again and again in the dressing room, while his teammates huddled around him. The football world had begged for one more special Pelé tournament – and he had delivered.

CHAPTER 21

TEARFUL GOODBYES

Pelé had made it clear that the 1970 final in Mexico would be his last ever World Cup game, but no one knew whether he would keep playing for Brazil over the next few years. He wasn't even sure himself. But there was more certainty with life at Santos as he returned from the World Cup glory in Mexico and prepared to chase trophies again.

Over the next few months, Pelé recalled Dondinho's advice about the beauty of walking away as a star and a winner, rather than waiting until there was nothing left to give. He also thought a lot about what it would mean to spend more time with his family after so many years of games, practices and travel. Eventually, he reached a decision on his international career.

'It's time for me to step away from the national team,' Pelé explained, as the news spread quickly around the world. 'It's been an honour to represent my country, and I'm so proud of the success we've had over the years. Now others will lead the way.'

Brazil's upcoming match against Yugoslavia, in July 1971, would be his last international game, and Pelé knew it was going to be an emotional day for everyone at the Maracanã – and for plenty more watching or listening around the world.

As he put on the famous yellow Number 10 shirt one last time, all the memories flooded back. He was happy and sad in the same moment, but most of all he was thankful for all the achievements on the pitch and all his incredible teammates over the years.

The crowd was standing and cheering from the minute that Pelé emerged from the tunnel for the warm-up, and the noise in the stadium got even louder once the game started, with 180,000 people making themselves heard.

'Stay! Stay! Stay!'

'King! King! King!'
'Pelé! Pelé! Pelé!'

Wow. When the ball went out for a throw-in, Pelé took the chance to look up around the stadium and savour the scene.

He could feel the love from the fans, and his whole body froze with all the overwhelming feelings. Leaving the field, the tears flowed down his cheeks and he couldn't stop crying. He waved and blew kisses to the crowd, as he took off his Brazil shirt for the last time.

Pelé agreed to play on at Santos for a few more years, but he knew that a similar emotional scene would lie ahead when he finished his club career. He had enjoyed so many wonderful seasons at Santos but the club was changing and it soon felt very different, with fewer familiar faces around.

Other teams began to take over in Brazil, winning the competitions that Santos had dominated for so many years. But Pelé was still scoring goals and keeping the team in contention. Santos won the Campeonato Paulista in 1973 and also found time to tour the globe more than ever, with trips to Europe,

Africa, Asia and Australia.

Finally, Pelé decided that it was time to hang up his boots, and he chose a game against Ponte Preta for his Santos goodbye, in October 1974.

As Pelé stood near the halfway line, ready for the kickoff, he could feel his heart racing. Just like his final Brazil game, his head was spinning and his legs felt like jelly. Memories of all the battles and all the trophies with Santos filled his thoughts. How was he supposed to play football when he was feeling like this?

He got a few early touches and the crowd roared each time. Then he saw a Ponte Preta midfielder chip the ball forward. Pelé instinctively took a couple of steps backwards, getting into position for a header at first, but at the last second he just put his arms up and caught the ball with his hands.

Everyone stopped. Even the referee looked confused and forgot to blow his whistle for a free kick. Pelé paused too and wasn't sure what to do next. It was too late to take back his handball. Instead, he just held the ball up above his head, and the whole stadium erupted in one giant cheer.

Pelé walked to the centre circle, put the ball down carefully and knelt over it, bowing to the fans who had cheered his name ever since he had arrived at the club in 1956. Once again, he was in tears as he said goodbye to his Santos family.

'What are we going to do without you?' Carlos Alberto said, also in tears. 'I can't believe this is the end.'

'It's been an incredible journey,' Pelé replied, hugging each of his teammates and coaches. 'I'm going to miss you all.'

Pelé had played nineteen seasons with Santos, scoring hundreds of goals for the club, and it would always have a special place in his heart.

As some Santos fans still pleaded with him to play another season, and others begged him to return to the Brazil team for future World Cups, the biggest question was: what was next for Pelé?

CHAPTER 22

ADVENTURES IN THE BIG APPLE

While Santos tried to move on without him, Pelé could finally turn his attention to retirement – no more training, no more travel, no more games. The extra family time was great, but he soon missed the excitement of being part of a team and competing week after week. He was still only thirty-five and he began to wonder if he had walked away from football too soon.

Then an offer arrived that gave Pelé even more to think about. The idea of moving to the United States and playing in the national league wasn't completely new, and he had given it some thought a few years earlier, but the timing was interesting when the New

York Cosmos approached him about joining the North American Soccer League (NASL).

'Come to America and you can win over a whole country,' they explained, laying out all the ways that 'soccer' was growing and how it was ready to make a big leap with the right star players onboard.

After all the years at Santos, Pelé had been sure that he would never play for any other club team. But this was a different type of opportunity and a new experience for the whole family. Why not?

'It's a chance to promote the game in the United States and I've got a few sponsorships there already,' he explained to his family. 'It would be really fun for us to explore New York together. Everyone says it's an amazing city.'

It wasn't an easy decision, but in the end Pelé agreed to a deal with the Cosmos and prepared to add one last chapter to his football career. He was still a huge celebrity and reporters from all over the world came to New York to be there for his first press conference.

'You can tell the world that soccer has finally arrived

in the USA,' Pelé announced with a big smile.

He was still smiling when he jogged onto the pitch in the Cosmos's all-white kit against the Dallas Tornado for his NASL debut. He got his own special introduction as the fans stood and cheered. But the first half was a disaster and the Cosmos were losing 2–0 at half-time.

Pelé was still getting to know his new teammates, but they already trusted anything he said about football. When he stood up in the dressing room, all eyes turned to him.

'This game isn't over,' he told them. 'The whole country is watching today to see what we can do, so let's put on a show in the second half.'

Pelé quickly got New York back into the game, setting up a goal with a perfect pass: 2–1.

Then the Cosmos won a free kick on the right wing. The New York players looked at Pelé to see if he wanted to take it, but he signalled that he would get into the box for the cross instead.

The ball was whipped in at just the right height and Pelé had a clear view of it. It was coming straight to him. He timed his jump perfectly and powered a header into the top corner, beating the keeper and the defender on the line.

Goooooooooooooooooooooaaaaaaaaaaaaaaaaalllllllllllllll lllllllllll!!!!!!!!!!!!!!!!!!!

'What a header!' shouted one of the Cosmos defenders, hugging Pelé as they celebrated in front of the screaming Cosmos fans. 'One day, I'm going to be telling my grandkids about this game!'

But the Cosmos didn't get close to a trophy in Pelé's first two seasons. He hated to lose, but he could see that his teammates were trying their best. Pelé was happy to stay for extra hours at training to work on drills with them and share some of his experience.

'We're better than this,' he said, trying to cheer up his teammates after one frustrating loss. 'Let's focus on the next game and win that one.'

Everything clicked in the 1977 season as New York lived up to their high expectations and reached the Soccer Bowl as one of the last two teams standing.

With chants of 'Pelé! Pelé!' floating around the stadium, the Cosmos took on the Seattle Sounders.

This was his chance to deliver a perfect New York ending to his time in the NASL.

Wearing the green Cosmos away shirt, Pelé felt confident, especially as New York had his old Brazil and Santos teammate Carlos Alberto as well as German star Franz Beckenbauer. Pelé dropped deep and often no Seattle defender went with him. That allowed him to turn and pick out a pass.

With the game locked at 1–1, Pelé started another quick attacking move. Left winger Steve Hunt whipped in the cross and striker Giorgio Chinaglia headed in the winning goal. Pelé jumped in the air and joined in the celebrations.

Pelé had the big trophy from his NASL adventure and now he felt able to walk away, with the Cosmos in a good place and the league growing in popularity.

All that was left was to arrange a testimonial match to give Pelé an official send-off. It would be Cosmos vs Santos at Giants Stadium in New York on 1 October 1977. Pelé would play forty-five minutes for each team and there was excitement from all corners of the world as the big day got nearer.

This was really it, this time. No more. Pelé was exhausted and ready for a proper break from football, but he was excited for this big occasion. His parents were both there, and star names like Muhammad Ali were in the crowd too.

Wearing the Cosmos shirt in the first half, Pelé lined up a free kick and laughed as he saw some of his old Santos teammates in the wall. He hit the ball hard, with just enough whip and dip to fly over the heads of the defenders and into the top corner.

Goooooooooooooooooooaaaaaaaaaaaaaaaallllllllllllll llllllllllll!!!!!!!!!!!!!!!!!!!

The crowd went wild. The singing and cheering swept around the stadium, and Pelé was the centre of attention one last time. He held up a Brazil and a United States flag as he was carried around the stadium one last time. Even in the pouring rain, nothing could wipe the smile off his face.

CHAPTER 23

THE LEGEND LIVES ON

His own football career was over but Pelé was still only in his late thirties and there was no way that he could just walk away from the game completely. So, after leaving New York and returning home to Brazil, he took some time to relax at last, then began to think about his future.

'So, am I looking at Santos' next coach?' Zoca teased.

Pelé shook his head. 'Oh no, you won't see me coaching,' he replied. 'But I still want to pay back the game of football for everything it's given me over the years. I just need to work out the best way to do that.'

First, he took on a Fair Play role with FIFA, working

hard to make changes and protect the game he loved. He also got more involved in projects as an ambassador to help promote football and charities around the world. In many ways, Pelé was still the face of the sport and he loved to use that for good causes. He even found time to be an actor in a film.

Free from the exhausting pressure of playing in World Cups, Pelé was still kicking and heading every ball as a Brazil fan. Somehow, he was more nervous watching the games now than he had been when he was playing in them! But the next few World Cups showed that the rest of the world had caught up. Brazil finished third in 1978, and then didn't get past the quarter-finals at the next three tournaments.

The 1994 World Cup was a different story, though. It was held in the United States and, of course, that meant there was a big Pelé connection after everything he had done to make football more popular there in his Cosmos days. It turned out to be a special summer as Brazil lifted the World Cup for the fourth time, but only after leaving Pelé biting his nails during a tense penalty shootout in the final.

After that tournament, Pelé felt it was time to focus his efforts on Brazil again. He had turned down a few opportunities to take on a bigger sports role back home, but in 1995 he decided to step up once again for his country by becoming Minister of Sports and helping to shape the future of football in Brazil.

Following in Pelé's footsteps, Brazil were still chasing more trophies. They reached the World Cup final again in 1998 but lost 3–0 to France. Four years later, Brazil were champions again, with Ronaldo firing the team to their fifth World Cup – the most ever – in a similar style to Pelé in 1970. That made Brazil the official football kings, but they would fall short at the next five tournaments despite having some very talented squads.

Away from football, Pelé continued to pick up awards for his contributions to the game. It says everything about Pelé the player and Pelé the person that his career was still being celebrated long after his playing days were over. As well as the many honours he was given in Brazil, he was also named a Citizen of the World by the United Nations and presented with a knighthood by the Queen of England.

'You're going to meet the Queen!' Zoca said with a big grin. 'That's amazing. Have you been practising your royal wave?'

Pelé laughed as Zoca did his best attempt at a fancy bow.

But as the years went by, Pelé's health got worse, and after a long illness, he died in December 2022. The football world came to a stop as players, past and present, digested the sad news.

'Pelé changed everything,' Neymar explained. 'He turned football into art, into entertainment. He is gone, but his magic will remain.'

Brazil announced three days of mourning, and hundreds of thousands of fans came to Santos to pay their respects at his funeral.

But the legend lives on. Pelé thrilled crowds all over the world in one of the greatest careers in the history of football – and his three World Cups, his glory years at Santos and all his remarkable records will never be forgotten.

The trophies are just part of the story, though. Pelé's

impact went far beyond that. His success put Brazil on the map as a football country and paved the way for so many others to achieve their dreams with the national team. From Zico and Sócrates, to Romário and Ronaldo, to Ronaldinho and Neymar, future generations looked up to Pelé as the hero who had set a whole new standard.

Pelé changed football forever and, for many, he will always be the greatest player that ever lived.

Read on for a sneak preview of
another brilliant football story by
Matt and Tom Oldfield. . .

VINÍCIUS JÚNIOR

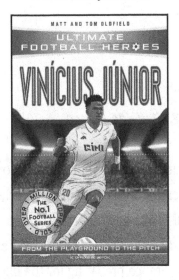

Available now!

CHAPTER 1

CHAMPIONS LEAGUE HERO

28 May 2022, Stade de France

When Vinícius Jr.'s alarm went off that morning,
he reached across for his phone and checked his
messages as if it was any other day. Except it wasn't.
Tonight would be the 2022 Champions League final
and he was in France preparing for the biggest game
of his life.

He sat up and stretched, shrugging off the nervous
feeling in his stomach. Ever since signing with
Real Madrid, 'Vini' had dreamed of winning the
Champions League. It was the trophy that everyone
talked about – and the photos were plastered on the

walls at the stadium, at the training ground and in just about every other corridor he could remember.

Zinedine Zidane. Raul. Luís Figo. Cristiano Ronaldo. Sergio Ramos. The list went on and on. So many Real Madrid legends had won that giant silver cup.

Vini put on his Real tracksuit and took the lift down to the huge hotel lobby. As the doors opened, he grinned at the familiar sight in the doorway of the team's meeting room. Real manager Carlo Ancelotti had the same calm face as always, and Vini immediately felt better. Carlo's belief in him had turned around his Real experience.

Once all the players had found a seat, Carlo and the coaches went through further instructions, using the big TV screens on the back wall. 'We know Liverpool are going to press us in midfield,' Carlo explained, looking at Luka Modrić and Toni Kroos. 'But we can play around it – just get the ball out to Vini as often as you can.'

All the reporters were talking about Vini's battle with Trent Alexander-Arnold, and he knew that the Liverpool right-back was great going forward but could sometimes lose concentration when forced to defend.

Vini listened carefully, but the clock in the meeting room seemed to be ticking more slowly than ever. He just wanted to get out on the pitch with a ball at his feet.

While the players left the room, picking up bottles of water on their way out, Vini stopped next to the whiteboard that showed the timing for the team bus ride to the stadium.

Carlo appeared out of nowhere. 'This is your moment,' he said, putting an arm round Vini. 'It's what you've worked so hard for. Now go and enjoy it!'

Vini laughed. He still remembered his first talks with Carlo and how he'd left the room each time feeling ten feet tall. All along, his manager had given him the freedom to be himself on the pitch. That meant playing with a smile and taking on defenders.

It was still hours before kickoff, but Vini could hear the screams of a large crowd of Real fans outside the hotel. As he boarded the bus, with his headphones tucked under his arm, he waved to them.

There were Real fans lining the streets along the

way, smiling and laughing. Almost all of them were wearing the club's famous white shirt.

During the warm-up for the game, Vini jogged over to join a circle of his teammates and flicked the ball around. His touch felt sharp as he moved from side to side – and standing next to Luka and Karim Benzema, he felt more confident that the night would end with the Champions League trophy in his hands.

'These finals are why we play the game,' Luka said, grinning. As usual, he was barely sweating. 'There's nothing else like it.'

Luka would know, Vini thought. He had already won the trophy four times.

Somehow the VINI JR 20 Real shirt, hanging in the dressing room, looked even more spectacular that night. Vini could feel the history and successes – and now he was following in the club legends' giant footsteps.

'It's almost time,' Carlo said quietly as the whole dressing room turned to listen. 'Everything about our journey to the final has felt magical. We were counted out against Chelsea and again when we were losing to

Manchester City. But we don't quit.'

Vini nodded as he taped his ankles.

In the tunnel, he closed his eyes, took a deep breath and said a quiet prayer. At last, he heard the tap-tap of studs on the tunnel floor and the line started moving.

The Champions League anthem blared out from the loudspeakers as Vini walked out onto the perfect green pitch.

'Let's go!' Karim shouted, high-fiving Vini on his way for the coin toss.

After the first few minutes, Vini felt the nerves disappear and his focus shifted to helping his team win the game. The first half was tight and no one wanted to make a big mistake.

'Just stick to the plan,' Carlo said at half-time. 'We're exactly where we want to be, and the chances will come. But when we get the ball wide, we've got to get more support in the box for Karim.'

In the second half, Real found their rhythm. A neat move on the right gave Federico Valverde some space. He took a quick touch and glanced up to check his options. Vini remembered Carlo's half-time words and rushed forward to support him.

Vini had played with Federico for years – from the Castilla reserve team all the way to the Real first team – and he could guess what was coming next. When Federico swung his right foot to whip the ball across the box, Vini was already on the move.

He timed his run perfectly, reacting faster than Alexander-Arnold. Vini's eyes lit up as Federico's cross-shot flew away from Allison, the Liverpool goalkeeper, and into his path. He slowed down just enough to side foot a quick shot into the net. *1–0!*

Goooooooooooooooooooaaaaaaaaaaaaaaaallllllllllllll llllllllllll!!!!!!!!!!!!!!!!!!!

Vini raced away towards the fans, grabbing the Real badge on his shirt and flashing his trademark smile. Was this really happening?! The crowd's reaction gave him a clear answer. Vini could hardly hear his teammates as they raced over and jumped on his back.

But Vini knew Liverpool wouldn't give up. He focused on getting back and helping the midfield. His heart skipped a beat a few times whenever Thibaut Courtois dived to make key saves.

He watched the final seconds from the bench, after a standing ovation from the fans and a hug from Carlo. Then it was all over! Vini leapt into the air and rushed onto the pitch to celebrate with his teammates.

'We did it!' he yelled, hugging Karim and Luka.

Standing in the line for his medal, Vini caught a glimpse of the shiny Champions League trophy. Real had won it as a team, but it still felt great to score the winning goal.

The past few years had been a whirlwind for Vini, with many highlights but some challenges and bumps. But now he really believed that anything was possible. He was still only twenty-one and he was just getting started.

CHAPTER 2

SÃO GONÇALO'S
GOLDEN BOY

As Little Vini looked out of the window, he saw a group of older boys making a goal with old milk cartons for posts. A scuffed, muddy ball pinged from one foot to the next when the boys ran around in the São Gonçalo street. It looked like fun!

With his focus on the football game, what Vini didn't see in that moment was the difficult surroundings in São Gonçalo – the dirty water, the rubbish on the ground and the lack of food. But he was already old enough to know that São Gonçalo could be dangerous.

His parents, Vinícius and Fernanda, had settled in this big, crowded neighbourhood, within the city of

Rio de Janeiro. They made the most of their family time, but life was hard.

There was a loud noise from just up the street, and Fernanda joined her son at the window nervously, looking left and right. The older boys had rushed off. They couldn't see anything, but Fernanda still guided Vini away from the window.

When Vini's parents weren't worrying about staying safe in São Gonçalo, they had money challenges to think about. There were so few jobs, and they had bills to pay.

'What are we going to do?' Fernanda asked, looking at her husband. 'How are we going to give our kids a better life?'

Vinícius didn't know. He hugged his wife. It would take a miracle.

'We'll find a way,' he said. 'Keep believing.'

'Always!' she said, smiling bravely and glancing over at their children. Vini was sitting on the floor next to his sister Alessandra and little brother Netinho.

The first task for Vinícius was finding a job. After weeks of searching, he got one, but it wasn't in São

Gonçalo. Every bit of good news seemed to have bad news attached to it. Now he would be away and would miss precious moments with his children.

As usual, they found a way to make it work, with help from the rest of the family. Sitting at the table one weekend, Vinícius and Fernanda were thankful for getting to the end of another long week.

'Coming through!' Vini called suddenly, whizzing past them with his little ball and almost tripping on a chair leg.

But he kept his balance, weaving in and out in the tiny space. When he got to the front door, he turned around and did the same run back through the house.

'Have you seen the way he dribbles his ball around?' Fernanda said, turning to her husband. 'Football could be his route out of here to a better life.'

'He's definitely a true Brazilian!' Vinícius replied, grinning. 'He loves watching the older kids playing in the street too. Before we know it, he'll be out there with them.'

There was a knock at the door, and Vinícius got up. 'That'll be Ulysses,' he said.

'Uncle Ulysses!' Vini shouted excitedly, after his dad had let him in.

Ulysses crouched down and tried to kick the ball away from Vini. But he was too slow. Vini spun around him laughing.

'The boy's got talent!' Ulysses said, giving up any hope of getting the ball. 'Have you looked at registering him for one of the local youth teams? There's only a very small fee and it'll keep him out of trouble.'

Vinícius and Fernanda looked at each other, smiling. 'We were actually just talking about his love of football,' Fernanda said.

'Well, think about it,' Ulysses replied. 'If you're interested, I can ask a few friends for suggestions on the local teams.'

'Yes please!' Vini called, rushing past them on another run. They all laughed.

When Ulysses got up to leave, Vini appeared out of nowhere, tapping the ball through his uncle's legs. 'Got you!' he said, giggling.

Hugging Vini at the door, Ulysses grinned. 'I'm

always telling your parents that you're welcome to come and stay with me any time,' he said. 'I'll be working on my goalie skills so I'm ready for you.'

Vini smiled. He liked going to see Uncle Ulysses and Auntie Tatiana. 'You're on!' he said.

PELÉ
HONOURS

Santos

🏆 South American Cup: 2012

🏆 Campeonato Paulista: 1958, 1960, 1961, 1962, 1964, 1965, 1967, 1968, 1969, 1973

🏆 Campeonato Brasileiro Série A: 1961, 1962, 1963, 1964, 1965, 1968

🏆 Copa Libertadores: 1962, 1963

🏆 Intercontinental Cup: 1962, 1963

🏆 Intercontinental Supercup: 1968

New York Cosmos

🏆 North American Soccer League, Soccer Bowl: 1977

Brazil

🏆 FIFA World Cup: 1958, 1962, 1970

Individual

🏆 FIFA World Cup Best Young Player: 1958

🏆 Campeonato Brasileiro Série A Top Scorer: 1961, 1963, 1964

🏆 Intercontinental Cup Top Scorer: 1962, 1963

🏆 Copa Libertadores Top Scorer: 1965

🏆 FIFA World Cup Golden Ball (Best Player): 1970

🏆 South American Footballer of the Year: 1973

🏆 NASL Most Valuable Player: 1976

🏆 International Peace Award: 1978

🏆 FIFA Order of Merit: 1984

🏆 World Team of the 20th Century: 1998

🏆 FIFA Player of the Century: 2000

🏆 FIFA Ballon d'Or Prix d'Honneur: 2013

PELÉ

18 THE FACTS

NAME: Pelé, or Edson Arantes Do Nascimento

DATE OF BIRTH: 23 October 1940

AGE: Died in 2022, aged 82

PLACE OF BIRTH: Três Corações

NATIONALITY: Brazil

CLUBS: Santos, New York Cosmos

POSITION: ST

THE STATS

Height (cm):	173
Club appearances:	1363
Club goals:	1281
Club trophies:	26
International appearances:	92
International goals:	77
International trophies:	3
Ballon d'Ors:	1

★ ★ ★ **HERO RATING: 95** ★ ★ ★

GREATEST MOMENTS

29 JUNE 1958,
BRAZIL 5–2 SWEDEN

On this unforgettable night, Pelé became Brazil's
Golden Boy and an international superstar. At the age
of only seventeen, he scored two great goals in the
World Cup final to lead his country to the trophy they
had been waiting years for. Brazil had their first World
Cup triumph and a football legend was born.

5 MARCH 1961, FLUMINENSE 1–3 SANTOS

In this match, Pelé picked up the ball near his own penalty area and dribbled all the way through to score, leaving seven Fluminense players on the floor. It was a goal so great that they even put up a special plaque for it: 'On this pitch, on March 5 of 1961, Pelé scored the most beautiful goal in the history of the Maracanã.'

11 OCTOBER 1962, BENFICA 2–5 SANTOS

Pelé was clearly brilliant in Brazil, but could he shine brightly against the best club teams in Europe as well? You bet! In this Intercontinental Cup final against Eusébio's excellent Benfica, Pelé showed that he was on another level. He led Santos to victory with two goals in the first leg and then three in the second – a hat-trick hero!

19 NOVEMBER 1969, VASCO DA GAMA 1–2 SANTOS

This was the moment that the whole of Brazil had been looking forward to – Pelé's 1000th goal, or 'O Milésimo' as it became known. In front of over 65,000 supporters at the famous Maracanã Stadium, he stepped up and scored the winner from the penalty spot. Hurray, he had done it! As the crowd clapped and cheered, Pelé was lifted into the air and carried on a mini victory lap.

21 JUNE 1970, BRAZIL 4–1 ITALY

Playing in his fourth and final World Cup, could Pelé fire Brazil to a third World Cup trophy? Of course he could! After scoring three goals in the earlier rounds, he then gave his team the lead in the final against Italy with a powerful, leaping header at the back post. What a moment and what a football hero!

TEST YOUR KNOWLEDGE

QUESTIONS

1. When little Edson and his family moved to Bauru, how did they travel there?

2. How did Pelé earn some extra money for the family when he was seven years old?

3. Who travelled with Pelé and Dondinho for the trial at Santos?

4. How old was Pelé when he signed with Santos?

5. How many goals did Pelé score in the 1958 World Cup Final?

6. True or false – Pelé also scored in the 1962 World Cup Final?

7. Who did Santos beat to win the 1962 Intercontinental Cup?

8. Who were Santos playing against when Pelé scored his 1,000th goal (O Milésimo)?

9. Which of Pelé's old teammates took over as Brazil manager just before the 1970 World Cup?

10. How many times did Pelé, as part of the Brazil squad, win the World Cup?

11. With which team did Pelé finish his career in the North American Soccer League?

Answers below . . . No cheating!

*1. By train. 2. Shining shoes. 3. Waldemar de Brito.
4. Fifteen. 5. Two! 6. False! Sadly, Pelé picked up an injury in Brazil's
second match and had to miss the rest of the tournament. 7. Benfica.
8. Vasco da Gama. 9. Mario Zagallo. 10. Three! (1958, 1962 and 1970).
11. New York Cosmos.*

PLAY LIKE YOUR HEROES

SCORE WORLD CUP-WINNING GOALS LIKE PELÉ

STEP 1: Well done, your team has reached a major football final! It's a huge achievement, but your biggest challenge is still to come. As the superstar striker, this is your time to shine... and score!

STEP 2: Pressure, what pressure?! Keep calm and keep doing what you do. Use your speed and brilliant football brain to make lots of dangerous runs behind the opposition defence. Because eventually, a golden chance will come...

STEP 3: ...and when it does, don't waste it. Believe in yourself and make the most of your hero moment!

STEP 4: If a teammate floats a pass towards you in the penalty area, THIS IS YOUR CHANCE! Be ready to pounce, and react in a flash. Chest the ball down, flick it over the head of the on-rushing defender, and then BANG! fire a powerful volley into the net.

STEP 5: If a teammate delivers a teasing cross into the box, THIS IS YOUR CHANCE! Move away from your marker and towards the ball. Watch it all the way onto your head and then BOOM! use your strong neck muscles to power the ball past the keeper. High or low, left or right – you choose, but always aim for a corner.

STEP 6: GOOOAAALLL!!! Hurray, you did it, hero! Make sure you enjoy your World Cup-winning moment to the max with all your teammates and supporters.

CAN'T GET ENOUGH OF
ULTIMATE FOOTBALL
HEROES?

Check out heroesfootball.com
for quizzes, games, and competitions!

Plus join the Ultimate Football Heroes
Fan Club to score exclusive content and
be the first to hear about
new books and events.
heroesfootball.com/subscribe/